A CATALOGUE OF MUSIC

by

AMERICAN MORAVIANS

1742-1842

From the Archives of the Moravian Church
at Bethlehem, Pa.

Compiled by

ALBERT G. RAU and HANS T. DAVID

AMS PRESS
NEW YORK

Reprinted from the edition of 1938, Bethlehem, Pennsylvania
First AMS EDITION published 1970
Manufactured in the United States of America

International Standard Book Number: 0-404-07206-2

Library of Congress Number: 76-134383

AMS PRESS INC.
NEW YORK, N.Y. 10003

CONTENTS

TABLE OF ABBREVIATIONS*

I. INDICATION OF PARTS

S   Soprano.

C   Canto (generally used for first and second soprano).

A   Alto (sometimes referred to as CA, Canto Alto).

T   Tenore.

B   Basso (often referred to as CB, Canto Basso, in contrast to an instrumental B).

1 or pr.   primo.

2 or sec.   secondo.

I (with vocal parts)   Coro primo.

II (with vocal parts) Coro secondo.

Vlo   Violino (*plural* Violi).

Vla   Viola.

Vlc.   Violoncello.

B   Basso (referring to a violoncello, or violoncello and bass, or both with organ).

Fl.   Flauto.

Ob.   Oboe.

Cl.   Clarinetto ("Clarino," which stands for the later trumpet, is always written out).

Fag.   Fagotto.

Co.   Corno.

Org.   Organo (including a reduction of the composition, unless stated differently).

II. INDICATIONS OF COPYISTS

PETER refers to John Frederick P., TILL to John Christian T., HERBST to John H., V VL to Jacob Van Vleck, G G M to George Godfrey Müller, DMM to David Moritz Michael and PW to Peter Wolle.

The following abbreviations are used for musicians who made copies but do not appear in the list of composers:

I N   Immanuel Nitschmann, b. Herrnhuth, 1736, came to America 1761, together with Dencke, d. at Bethlehem, 1791. He wrote most of the early Bethlehem manuscripts. His second wife was a sister of Van Vleck.

II W   Hannah Weber, b. at Bethlehem, 1763, organist in the Sister's House, d. at Bethlehem, 1840. She served as professional copyist, for Church diaries as well as music.

C F S   Christian Frederick (Friedrich) Schaaff, b. Berthelsdorf, 1759, came to America, 1795, overseer of the married people, succeeding Dencke, singing teacher of the children, went to Salem 1819, d. there 1841. He furnished most of the doubling parts to compositions by Peter and others.

While there is no doubt about the handwriting of HERBST and H W, and very rarely about those of PETER, TILL, BECHLER, G M M, I N and C F S, it must be stated that the attribution of copies to V VL, DMM and PW is sometimes questionable.

HERBST and GGM always refer to manuscripts from LITITZ, all the others to such from BETHLEHEM, unless other indications are given.

All manuscripts mentioned in the present catalogue are now either at the Moravian Archive or at the Central Moravian Church, both at Bethlehem; the indications BETHLEHEM, LITITZ, NAZARETH, LANCASTER therefore refer to the place from which the manuscripts were taken, not to their present location. The catalogues of the LANCASTER and GRACEHAM collection also are preserved at Bethlehem.

---

* The P. after incomplete German titles is used in the originals. It stands there for *perge* (continue).

PREFACE

This list of anthems composed in America by musicians belonging to the Unitas Fratrum or Moravian Church has been prepared under a generous appropriation by The American Philosophical Society to the Moravian Seminary and College for Women. The manuscripts are preserved in the Archives of the Moravian Church at Bethlehem, Pennsylvania, and comprise more than two thousand separate items collected from the musical life of the congregations at Bethlehem, Lititz, Lancaster, and Nazareth in Pennsylvania, and Winston-Salem, North Carolina. Quite naturally the large part of this mass of material consists of works composed in Europe by musicians, Moravians and otherwise, during the last half of the eighteenth and the beginning of the nineteenth centuries. But this project has revealed the very large quantity of original work done by these people in America, and now exposes the incompleteness of the accounts of the early development of music in our land.

The Moravian settlements in the colonies began at Bethlehem in 1742. They were founded as centers of missionary effort among the Indians, and as nuclei for church concentration for the many German migrants to Pennsylvania. Each one of these villages was a planned "gemein ort" whose inhabitants were carefully picked on the Continent and in England with reference to their ability to assist in "the plan." The scheme was fathered and financed by Count Nicholas von Zinzendorf from his home at Berthelsdorf in Saxony and from his temporary residence in London.

It is not to be wondered at, therefore, that many of the leaders, artisans and workers in the group should have been more or less trained in music and have been competent performers on various musical instruments. The Diary of the Bethlehem settlement is full of descriptions of song services, accompanied by violins, flutes and horns. There are references in those lines to the use of spinets and organs in the community houses and the church. A small orchestra was founded in 1748 under the leadership of John Westmann, called the Collegium Musicum, that continued its musical efforts for over half a century. In 1754 a complete choir of trombones, in four voices, was imported and has been maintained to the present time.

All of this musical effort, however, was directed solely toward the enrichment of the evangelical spirit, and while these allusions to music in the diary are plentiful, at no time do they specify *what* music was performed.

As nearly as we can determine, the chorales of the Reformation time and antiphonal chanting of liturgies, formed the sole musical pabulum for twenty years after the foundation of the town. Probably this was the type of music that Franklin heard in 1755 when he lived in Bethlehem for a few weeks, to which he makes reference in his diary.

Nor have we found in this project any manuscript that is earlier than 1766, though the diary records that J. C. Pyrlaeus and C. F. Oerter composed "cantatas" for liturgical purposes as early as 1747.

The musical life of which we have found manuscript record begins with the coming of Jeremiah Dencke in 1761. Dencke introduced solo and chorus anthems into the services, some of which he brought from Europe, and some that he composed here. He makes use of strings, flutes, and horns in his scores, thus confirming our hyphothesis that there had been a previous period of development. After Dencke there arrived in succession John Frederick Peter, Simon Peter, John Herbst, Sr., John Herbst, Jr., Jacob Van Vleck, John Christian Till, David Michael, John Cunow, John Bechler, Peter Wolle, Francis Hagen, and Peter Ricksecker. Every one of these men was either a clergyman or a worker in the schools of the church establishment. Five of them, Van Vleck, Till, Hagen, Wolle, and Ricksecker, were born on this continent. Three of them were Bishops of the church. To all of them their music was a side issue in the greater job of spreading the Gospel of Christ.

This may account for the fact that we find so little of secular music in their left overs. A number of home made methods for the spinet and organ, with exercise books, and a treatise on harmony in manuscript by Bishop Herbst, are our sole hints as to how this music tradition was carried on. J. F. Peter composed six quintettes for strings that are original in conception and clever in form. D. M. Michael wrote more than a dozen "Parthien" for wind instruments and a symphony, which latter, as far as we can find, has been lost. Hagen, too, composed an overture which is here in manuscript.

The oldest American manuscript we found is a Liturgy for the Synod of 1766, by Dencke. It is followed by special services for the Choir Festival of the "Older Girls," 1767, and for the Christmas services, 1767, also by Dencke. From that time on there is a steady succession of liturgies and anthems for all seasons of the church year and for all sorts of sacramental occasions.

Because of the fact that the administration at Bethlehem constantly changed the place of service of its workers, some of these compositions were written at Nazareth, Lititz, Lancaster, and Salem. But in nearly every case copies are found in the Bethlehem collection.

All of the works in this catalogue have been found in complete manuscript shape: voices, organ, orchestra parts. The Salem archives contains a group of four hundred full scores, once the property of Bishop John Herbst. Many of these he brought from Europe in 1784 and of course they are not native works. But, evidently, while he was pastor at Lititz, he added many new works of his own and copied those of his contemporaries. However, there are less than ten titles in the Salem Catalogue that are not available in manuscripts at Bethlehem.

While the gathering of this large mass of manuscripts from dusty church attics and cupboards occupied many years, the actual spade work of classification was done by Dr. Hans T. David, whose technical equipment and whose enthusiasm for the work made him invaluable. We owe thanks, too, to the New York Public Library, and particularly to Dr. Carlton Sprague Smith, for advice and help of all kinds. Through his interest in the project, black line prints of many of these compositions are now available through the New York Public Library in a series entitled *Music of the American Moravians.*

We wish also to acknowledge the assistance of the Rev. Dr. Wm. N. Schwarze, the Rev. Kenneth Hamilton, both of the Bethlehem Archives, and of Dr. Adelaide Fries of the Archives, Winston-Salem, N. C.

ALBERT G. RAU.

Bethlehem, July 4, 1938.

THE BEGINNINGS OF ORIGINAL MUSIC AT BETHLEHEM AND LITITZ

Jeremiah Dencke was born at Langenbilau, Silesia, Oct. 2, 1725. He became organist at Gnadenfrei and then, in 1748, at Herrnhut. He served as *Brüderpfleger* (overseer of the single brethren) at Gnadenberg, was ordained a deacon at Herrnhut. May, 1758, by John de Watteville, and in 1759 stationed at Zeist, Holland. In 1761, he came to America together with Johann Friedrich Peter, the father of the musicians, Johann Friedrich and Simon Peter, and with Immanuel Nitschmann.

Dencke was first Brüderpfleger at Christiansspring near Nazareth, then warden of the Bethlehem congregation, 1772, which important office he held, during the war, until 1784. He was made pastor successively at Bethlehem, Lititz, Nazareth and again Bethlehem. He finally worked as overseer of the married people at Bethlehem, from 1793 until his death, May 28, 1795. He married first in Bethlehem, 1771, then in Lititz, 1789; his third wife, Elizabeth Leinbach, born in Oley, Pa., survived him.

Dencke's outstanding musical ability is proven by the fact that he was considered worthy to be organist at Herrnhut. It would seem that he was the first Moravian to write concerted church music in America. Most of Dencke's compositions are preserved in scores written by Johann Friedrich Peter, who was to become the brother-in-law of Dencke through the latter's third wife. All the compositions copied by Peter are for a soprano solo with strings and, presumably, organ. A few of these were used later on as choruses. In addition to the compositions preserved, five more are mentioned in the oldest Bethlehem catalogue, which, however, are lost. The titles are:

Ach banne völlig jeden Hang

Herrliche Dinge werden in dir gepredigt

Komm, edler Held, du Held aus Davids Stamm

Sein Ruhen in der Erden (also in Graceham catalogue)

Welch ein sanftes Friedenswehen

Other compositions, which are attributed to Dencke in catalogues of Winston-Salem, were probably written by his son, Christian Frederick Dencke (b. at Bethlehem, Sept. 8, 1775; d. at Salem, Jan. 12, 1838). It would seem that Dencke quitted composition in his later years.

While no compositions written by Moravians in America are known to be older than Dencke's, and while undoubtedly he was the first to create music of a high rank, it is quite possible that, to a certain extent, original musical work was done before he arrived. The Bethlehem Archive preserves a series of compositions in an arrangement for voices, strings, one or two harps and an occasional harpsichord. These compositions were, as far as their origins could be traced, composed in Europe, but apparently adapted for the use of the Sister's House. The title page of one of these manuscripts is reproduced at the end of this volume, Plate A. The parts for the harps are at places so independent from the voices we may assume that they made use of original parts for wind instruments. No date is known for these arrangements which might go back into the sixties or even further.

The material from Lititz includes a small pile of parts not catalogued by Herbst. There are four bindings with the headings Canto I, Canto II, Alto and Basso; to these belonged apparently an organ part which is completely lost. The contents are partly still included, partly scattered. Many more single parts of the same size, and in the same handwritings apparently belong to the same group of manuscripts, which were used before Herbst entered the musical life at Lititz. Dates range from 1772 to 1780. The handwriting of G. G. Miller and, rarely, of J. F. Peter appears in some of the later pieces. The character of the festivals mentioned leads to the conclusion that these parts also came from the Sister's House. They include fragments of compositions by men who arrived in America several years before Dencke, although the compositions themselves do presumably not antedate most of Dencke's known works.

Matthias Gottfried Hehl, born April 30, 1705, at Ebersdorf, Württemberg, Magister Artium of the University of Tübingen, was ordained a bishop of the Church in 1750, and came to America in the following year. He participated in the corner-stone laying of Nazareth Hall on May 3, 1755, and is said to have deposited a hymn of his own in it. In the following years he came to Lititz and remained there until his death, Dec. 4, 1787. This "profound theologician, eloquent preacher, gifted musician and fine hymnologist" is represented in the manuscripts mentioned, by a *Cantata Hallelujah! Preis Ehr und Macht p. Autore Mattheo* in F major. It fills two pages at the beginning of the Canto I. This part is called *Chorus II. Vox prima continua.* During the first section, 2/4, 15 meas., *Munter und mit heller Stimme,* the second chorus rests: *Diese 15 tacte zu pausiren da indessen das Erste Chor 7 mal Hallelujah singt.* The second section, 2/4, 22 meas., again set to the word *Hallelujah,* includes a short Basso solo, presumably just an imitation after which the indica-

tion *Langsam und herzhaft* is given and a postlude of 3 meas. The
third section, 2/4, 26 meas., introduces the rest of the text,
Preis Ehr und Macht p., and toward the end is marked *Langsam
und pathetisch,* including a postlude of 4 meas. A hymn, 2/2, 11
meas. in G maj., *Der uns mit seinem Blut erkauft,* follows *Chor-
alisch mit Affect.* Unfortunately no other parts are preserved.
The composition, which is melodically attractive, was presumably written around 1772.

Another composition in the same handwriting, shows the re-
mark of A. R. Beck, *M. Hehl's writing—probably his composition.*
It is set likewise for two choruses, 2/4, 29 meas., G maj. The text
starts *Heilig, selig, Herz erfreulich und gedeihlich ist die
Freundschaft und Gemeinschaft die wir haben.* After 17 meas.,
Hehl indicates *Laut u. lieblich.* The last 6 are given to a postlude.
The part preserved is again the Soprano of the second choir.

A third composition in the same handwriting, and presumably
also of Hehl's composition gives a setting of the words *Ach Gott!
mein Lämmlein! Ich bin ein armer Sünder p.* It is set in F maj.,
has two verses of 12, 16 and 16 meas. each, in 2/4. Very possibly
the text as well as the music was written by Hehl. Only a Canto
primo is preserved.

Bernhard Adam Grube, born at Walschleben, near Erfurt, in
1715, studied theology at Jena, was ordained a deacon in 1740,
and came to Pennsylvania in 1748. He worked as a missionary
among the Indians. He too attended the laying of the corner-
stone for Nazareth Hall, and is said to have deposited a hymn
in the Delaware language. He went to Lititz, as minister, in
1763, served later at various places, and died at Bethlehem, in
1808.

One of the sheets mentioned above bears the note of A. R.
Beck: *All of this music is in the hand of the Rev. Bernard Adam
Grube.* A series of 4 compositions *Zum Led. Schww. Fest 1774*
indicated as being *di Grube.* The first one *Wohl dem, der du
erwählet p.*, a simple composition in F maj., written without any
flats, has 17 meas., C. The second *Die gepflanzt sind in dem
Hause des Herrn p.*, in D maj. has 35 meas., 3/4. The third one
Wohl dir, du hast es gut p. is kept in the style of a Liturgy (see
the notes below), without barlines, filling 13 measures of 2/2,
alla breve (4/2), in C maj. The last one ——, *Munter* in, starts
with a rest of 10 meas. It is incompletely handed down. Of these
compositions the C pr. as well as the C sec. were found. The
musical value of the compositions is not considerable.

The word "Liturgy" will often appear on the following pages.
It seemed advisable to explain this type of composition here.

The *Liturgie* represents the earliest type of service used in the
renewed Church of the Brethren. Originally these liturgies were

intended as complete services. Many of the early liturgies were designed or written by Count Zinzendorf. The earliest edition of the texts of the liturgies was published in 1770 as *Liturgische Gesänge der evangelischen Brüdergemeinden*. Another edition was printed at Barby in 1791, *aufs neue revidiert und vermehrt*. This edition is handed down in several copies one of which was signed by *Johann Jacob Schmidt July den 28 ten 1794*.

The liturgus, chorus and congregation generally alternate in presenting the liturgies. The liturgus sings with organ accompaniment, in a simple declaiming style. The chorus is written in 4 parts mostly note against note; the style of these parts reminds that of the Lutheran litany. The congregation is supposed to insert fitting chorales.

The earliest compositions of liturgies were probably made by Gregor. Peter copied liturgies by *Gregor und Francke* in 1779. After the revised edition of the book of liturgies was published the liturgies included in it were simply quoted by numbers. Several of these were composed by Christian Gottlieb Hueffel (b. 1762, d. 1842) who lived in Bethlehem, 1818-1826.

The singing of liturgies must be considered as one of the most important musical activities of the Moravians. The diaries, especially those Herbst kept, frequently mention the liturgies sung. Their performance may have partly replaced the singing of hymns in one or several languages which is recorded from the time of the first settlers at Bethlehem. Musically the litanies do not offer much of special interest. The earliest liturgies use instruments in unison. Later on modest interludes of the instruments are inserted.

JEREMIAH DENCKE'S COMPOSITIONS

Doxologie Zum Eingang des Provincial Synodi in Bethlehem, 1766.

HErr, unser Gott! der du uns gemacht hast zu deinem Volk und zu Schafen Deiner Weide p.

2/2 (Alla breve), B flat maj.

This liturgy is the earliest composition proven to be written in Bethlehem. It is a dignified work, melodically more attractive than one should expect from a composition in so restricted a style. Occasional interludes are well placed and written. The first page of the C pr. is reproduced in facsimile at the end of this catalogue, Plate B.

MANUSCRIPT. I N—C pr., C sec., C tertio (in alto clef), CB, Vlo I, II, Vla, B, Org. (figured bass). Fol.

No. 61.

PARTITUR
EINER MUSICK ZUM MÄDGEN-FEST
D. 25n MERZ 1767.

1.

Meine Seele erhebet den HErrn p.

Moderato 2/2, 28 meas. Prel. 6, interl. 3 and 3, postl. 3.

The three series of compositions handed down in scores of J. F. Peter, which are described on the following pages include exclusively solos for a soprano with 4 strings and presumably organ. The organ part of these pieces was probably played in the manner of accompaniment improvised from a figured bass. Peter in copying from the original parts did not include the figures.

The soli differ greatly in style and character. The present one offers a striking combination of elements of the recitative and the chorale with a concerted accompaniment. It is included in the first volume of the Music of the American Moravians together with the following compositions and the last one written for the same occasion.

2.

Ich will singen von einem Könige p.

Lieblich mit Affect. 2/2, 34 meas. Prel. 12, postl. 8 meas. B fl. maj.

Etwas mässiger, 26 meas. Interl. 6 meas., postl. 2 meas. g min. up to the end of the interl. then B fl. maj.

A regular Aria, with a contrasting middle section, but no actual recapitulation.

3. (No. 7.)

Freuet euch, ihr Töchter Seines Volks p.

Andante 3/4, 90 meas. Prel. 26, interl. 7, postl. 7. F maj.

This rather extended aria, less inspired than the others, gives a true picture of Dencke's technical facility.

4. (No. 8.)

Gehe in den beruch deines Bräutigams.

Con affetto 3/2, 56 meas. Prel. 5, interl. 2 and 2., postl. 2 meas.

Lente 25 meas. Postl. 1 meas. B fl. maj. The first section ending, the Lente beginning in g min.

This Aria, a quite dignified composition, gives a good contrast against the preceding one. Especially the codetta, approximately in the style of a chorale, deserves attention.

MANUSCRIPT. Score written by *C. F. Peter d.9n Febr. 1778.* *1)* p. 2-3, 2.) p. 3-5, 3.) p. 6-8, 4.) p. 9-11. No indication is made as to what pieces were left out in this copy.

No. 62.

PARTITUR
ZUR CHRISTNACHT-MUSIC DER KINDER 1767

1.

Siehe ich komme, im Buch ist von mir geschrieben.

Text con Affetto 3/4, 36 meas. Prel. 15, postl. 10. G maj.

Opening Aria of an unusual form, inasmuch the solo voice is introduced only for the short middle section. Effective setting. The present composition is reproduced at the end of this catalogue, Plates C-D.

2.

Uns ist ein Kind geboren p.

Text Grave 2/2, 51 meas. Prel. 15, post. 11 (dal segno meas. 5). D maj.

An Aria typical for Dencke's style in which the solo part is free from florid ornaments. The expressive composition gives an excellent continuation and sufficient contrast to the previous number.

3.-5. (A series of Arias using the same setting.)
Stört nicht meinen sanften Frieden p.

No. 3. Aria con Sordini. Liebl. spielend und mässig 2/4, D maj.

After a prelude of 16 meas. the voice offers twice a song in two part form. The first section ends in the dominant after 15 meas., the second in the tonic after 26, the last 6 of which are set as an instrumental postl. The melodic line is simple and touching.

No. 4. *Kindlein voller Gnadentriebe p.*

Senza Sordini. Aria Vers 3.

A slightly varied repetition of the preceding number. The interludes are changed.

No. 5. *Nimm Du meiner Seel Verlangen p.*

Senza Sordini, aber doch sehr piano.   Aria Vers 4.

Another variation to the same Air. The end of the vocal part leads effectively to the higher octav of the original tonic. The postlude is augmented to 8 meas.

6.

O welch unerhörtes Lieben p.

Arietta 3/4, twice 10 meas., and 26, the last 6 of which are instrumental. D maj.

Another rather popular Air which concludes adequately the earliest Christmas music composed at Bethlehem of which we know. The beginning resembles that of God save the King. The composition with the word *Jesus der so gerne regnet* is also handed down on a single sheet, in E flat maj. with the date 22n May 1759. Here solo part and keyboard accompaniment are given in 2 staves. In 1759, Dencke was still in Europe.

MANUSCRIPT. Score written by *Joh. Fr. Peter d. 11. Febr. 1778.* The single pieces are written on p. 1.) 3-4, 2.) 4-5, 3.) 6-7, 4.) 8-9, 5.) 10-11, 5.) 12. Instrumental parts No. I/II, Vla, B) to 2. anthem by H. Weber, together with Siehe ich verkundige by Grimm and Ehre Sey Gott p. (Glory to God) by Gregor. See also next number.

No. 64.

PARTITUR

ZUR CHRISTNACHTS-MUSIC DER GEM(EINDE) 1768

1.

Mache dich auf, werde Licht p.

Lebhaft 3/2. 42 meas. Prel. 16, interl. 2, postl. 5. C maj.
A short Aria of majestic character. Excellent use is made of syncopations in the instruments.

2.

Denn siehe, Finsternis bedecket das Erdreich p.

Ernsthaft 3/2, 13 meas. a min. Freudig 18 meas.
This number is in fact a second part to the preceeding. The first section with a more declaiming character and interludes of 1 and 2 measures in the manner of an accompanied recitative

has the function of a middle section. It is concluded with a striking postlude of 4 meas. The last section begins as a free recapitulation of No. 1. It starts in C maj. and ends with a postl. of 5 meas. in G maj.

3.

Machet die Thore weit und die Thüren in der Welt hoch p.

Freudig 3/4, 29 meas. Postl. 4 meas. G maj.
Short Aria of less special interest.

4.

Wer ist derselbe König der Ehren?

Solo col Orgo, 2/2, 6 meas. Transition to introduce the text of the following piece. G maj.

Es ist der HErr, stark und mächtig p.

Mit Affect con Spirito 3/2, 30 meas., 2/2, 2 meas. D maj. modulating to G maj. Another striking composition, made lively by dotted quarters with eighth notes and fine, melodic use of the triads. Several interludes are given, including one of 3 and one of 2 meas. The section in triple time is concluded by a postlude of 5 meas. The word Selah is sung twice with the cadence in alla breve time at the end.

5.

Grave 2/2 Anfang siehe vorj(ährige) Kinder Music.

The No. 2 of No. 62 is sung completely. Then the conclusion is given with:

Er heisset der Wunderbare p.

3/2, 28 meas. 4 interl. of 2 and 3 meas., postl. 4. G maj.
The piece would be effective were it not for the exaggerated use of triple time in the entire series. In the present section triplets are used at several places.

MANUSCRIPTS.

Score by *Joh. Fr. Peter d. 12n Febr. 1778* including 1.) on p. 2-3, 2 on p. 4, 3.) 5, 4.) 6-7, 5.) 8-9, p. 10-12 being left blank.

Parts in ''Music zu Weyhnachten 1772,'' fol. No. 15.

These parts, possibly in Dencke's hand, include:

No. 1. Singet dem HErrn ihr Kinder Zion di Graun

No. 3. Zion hörts und ist froh

No. 5. Machet die Thore weit. The composition mentioned above in a setting for Chorus.

2tes Chor. Wer ist derselbe König der Ehren? (music not included)

Es ist der HErr! starck und mächtig p. Dencke's composition in 4 part setting, First section (14 meas.)

Machet die Thore weit p. Another composition. 3/4 7 meas., 2/2 12 meas. Possibly a continuation made by Dencke

Kinder. Zeuch in unsre Herzen p. (no music)

2tes Chor. Wer ist derselbe König der Ehren? (as above)

Es ist der HErr Zebaoth p. Last section of Dencke's composition, including Selah

No. 7. Uns ist ein Kind geboren. Dencke's composition, in 4 part setting, arranged for 2 antiphonal choruses

Singet dem HErrn alle Lande p.

C pr., C sec., A, CB for Nos. 1 and 3 only; Vlo I/II, Vla, is by I N; Organ parts to 1, 8, 3 later.

In allen Dingen lasset uns beweisen als die Diener Gottes.

Moderato 2/4, 56 meas. Prel. 15, interl. 8, postl. 8 meas. e min.

One of the few choruses by Dencke we know. The choral setting is simple, but well done. The comparatively long instrumental sections are quite attractive. The second entrance of the chorus is set in the related major. The composition appears within a set of 7, the first three of which are by Gregor. The fourth is Peter's Duett Es ist ein Köstlich Ding, composed in 1772, the fifth by an unknown composer. Dencke's composition is the sixth, being followed by Peter's O Chor des Herrn, which was also written in 1772. The organ part includes for most pieces a figured bass only, but full accompaniment for the Ariette No. 5. Both the string parts and the organ part include chorales, to be sung by the congregation, or, as the organ indicates, occasionally by a solo voice.

MANUSCRIPT. C pr., C sec., A, CB, Vlo I/II, Vla, B, Org. fol.

Gesegnet bist du mein Volk p.

Affectuoso 2/2, 48 meas. Prel. 14, postl. 11 meas. C maj.

Regular anthem, with extended instrumental sections, but not outstanding. This composition is handed down with the material from Lititz. It seems that the indication on the title page "di JDencke" was made by Dencke himself. The handwriting of this signature, however, does not conform with that of the title page itself and the music. The Lititz collection includes several compositions in the same handwriting as the present one. As these pieces are not mentioned in Herbst's catalogue it is extremely difficult to determine their author. Probably they were written at Lititz before Herbst came there, but are not by Dencke.

MANUSCRIPT. C pr., C sec., CA, CB, Vlo I/II, Vla, B.

JOHN FREDERICK PETER

John Frederick Peter, or as he used to call himself, Johann Friedrich Peter, was born at Heerendijk in Holland, of German parents, May 19, 1746. His father, also called Johann Friedrich Peter, served as Moravian minister there, and was, in 1760, called as minister to Bethlehem. The younger Johann Friedrich lost his mother early, and was first sent to the children's institution at Haarlem, which afterwards was removed to Zeist, later to a similar institution at Niesky which in turn was removed to Hennersdorf. In 1760 the Pädagogium was removed to Niesky where Johannes von Watteville became of great influence on Peter. In 1765, Peter entered the Seminarium at Barby, and in 1770, he came to America.

Peter arrived at Bethlehem on May 18, 1770, and left after a few days for Nazareth where he served as teacher of the little boys. He returned to Bethlehem on January 30, 1773, and stayed there for 6 years, keeping the Church diary and attending to other similar duties. In September, 1779, he left for Lititz where he spent half a year. In May of the following year he went to Salem, North Carolina, where he was ordained a deacon shortly after his arrival. He remained in the Southern Province for ten years, serving for more than two as a minister "ad interim" at Salem. He married, in 1786, Catharina Leinbach from Oley, Pa., a sister of Dencke's third wife. She is said to have been the leading soprano of the Salem Church choir.

From September, 1790, until April, 1791, Peter worked at Graceham, Maryland. He passed through Bethlehem to serve in Hope, New Jersey, for two years. In December, 1793, he finally returned to Bethlehem. He spent there the rest of his life, except for a two years' sojourn in the small settlement at Montjoy. He died at Bethlehem, 1813.

Peter was undoubtedly the most gifted among the American Moravians. A fuller account of his work and character has been given by Albert G. Rau, in Musical Quarterly, July, 1937. Since then, a number of Peter's compositions have been found. They prove that Peter had started composing almost immediately after he came to America, in 1770. While his first steps were taken very cautiously, it would seem that Christian Gregor, the famous organizer of Moravian music, who visited the American province from 1770 to 1772, had encouraged him. Peter copied a large number of compositions by Gregor in score, between September,

1773, and April, 1774. Apparently Gregor sent his manuscripts after he had returned to Germany. All these compositions were written in the years 1760 to 1764. They include the *Freuden-Music zum Friedens-Danck-Feste d.21n Merz 1763* which is mentioned in O. Sonneck's Bibliography of early American secular music. Whoever furnished Sonneck with the information about this score, overlooked that Gregor is clearly indicated as the author.

The following list of Peter's compositions attempts a chronological order. The works in question form four different groups which can easily be separated. The first group includes those works which are handed down in copies made before Peter returned from the Southern Province. Most of these are handed down in score, and nearly all of them are dated. All scores mentioned are written by Peter himself. A second group is formed by those compositions which include a single set of vocal parts only. Later on, Peter could count on a choir so large that at least a double set of vocal parts was necessary. At the same time, he had a larger number of woodwind instruments at his disposal. Around 1800, Peter started to write compositions of a larger scope, for which he used unvariably sheets in folio size, in contrast to the earlier compositions which were throughout written on paper in octavo, and to a group of more modest later compositions, which are again written on paper of smaller size.

Within the groups, chronological order is maintained by using the oldest call numbers of the compositions. The oldest catalogue of music in Bethlehem is a *Verzeichniss der Gemein Musicalien auf Bethlehem,* made for, and now preserved at Winston-Salem. It is alphabetically arranged, and mentions the names of the composers. A similar catalogue of compositions at Nazareth, which, however, does not mention names of composers, is also found in Winston-Salem. The Bethlehem catalogue mentions 10 compositions by Peter only; these are put here at the beginning of the second group, unless they are already mentioned in the first. A second catalogue was made by C. F. Schaaff and H. Weber. This catalogue is the oldest to give call numbers of the compositions. It was made before the earliest numbers of the compositions were changed, and it is this catalogue from which the numbers at the head of the following compositions are taken. Later on, the numbers were changed several times, in the manuscripts as well as in the catalogue, and it is sometimes hard to find out the original numbers which, to a certain extent, represent a chronological order.

While the first catalogue represents the state of the Church Library around or before 1800, the second may be dated around 1815. A third one which was made by C. F. Schaaff and, like the second one, supplemented by Till, and others, gives the complete text for all compositions, and indicates the festivals for which they were written. There are several other catalogues, made in later years for the use of the choir. It did not seem advisable to include all numbers found in these catalogues. Most of the old manuscripts are now in the Moravian Archive at Bethlehem, alphabetically arranged. There are, however, a number of anthems which are still in use at the Church, and the manuscripts of these are preserved at the Library of the Central Moravian Church, arranged according to call-numbers. The call-numbers for these which are marked by an ''A'' are given in parentheses together with the description of the manuscripts.

The present catalogue includes 56 anthems by Peter, in addition to the 6 quintets for strings which Peter composed while at Salem. 21 of the anthems are also mentioned in catalogues of the collections at Winston-Salem. The same catalogues include 26 more titles of compositions by Peter. How many of these are actually preserved, nobody knows. It is highly probable that none of the compositions alluded to, were composed after 1790. As Peter neither copied these compositions nor had them copied later on, nor took them with him when he went back North, as he did with the Quintets and the score No. 145/149, we may conclude that he did not pay much attention to these works, whereas we find later compositions by Peter of which he made 2 or even 3 copies of his compositions. In the Bethlehem catalogues, there are scarcely any compositions by Peter listed which are not preserved, in contrast to such of Dencke, Herbst and others.

In his later years Peter used to write for a double chorus. One set of parts would consist of S, A, T, B, the other of Canto primo (Soprano I), Canto secondo (Soprano II) and Alto. As no boys were used in the regular church choir, the first chorus must have been a mixed one, while the second was one of women's voices. At this time, the separation of the sexes to which R. A. Grider refers apparently was no more strictly observed. But as the married women were, according to Grider, allowed to sing solos at an earlier period than the unmarried, the ''Single Sisters.'' it is quite probable that the high voices in the mixed chorus were performed by married people, while the women's chorus was entirely made up by single sisters.

While in earlier times Immanuel Nitschmann and Jacob Van Vleck united to make sets of copies it must be stated that Peter rarely had any assistance. The copies made by H. Weber, C. F. Schaaff and J. C. Till must in any case be considered as later additions to the parts written by Peter himself.

I.

PETER'S EARLY COMPOSITIONS
1770-1790

No. 27.

Partitur einiger Stücke
d. 14t May, 1774

Holograph score of 20 pages, the music starting on p. 2. The first four numbers were composed for festivals from 1770 to 1772. They fill 12 pages of the score, which are folded together. The other compositions, composed in 1773 are copied on a second booklet of 8 pages. Whether Peter has added the latter and the title-page in 1774, or copied the entire score in 1774, is hard to say, but the appearance of the score leads to the conclusion that the manuscript was entirely written in 1774.

1. Zum 13n Jul. 1770.
LEITE MICH IN DEINER WAHRHEIT P.

Andante 2/2, 24 meas. B fl. maj. Langsam 3/4, 14 meas. E fl. maj.

Peter arrived in Bethlehem May 18, 1770. On May 28 he went to Nazareth as teacher of the boys at Nazareth. The present composition apparently is the first one he composed in Colonial America, and very possibly the first one he ever attempted to write. The modesty with which he approached the new task is significantly displayed in all compositions included in the present score, but they prove at the same time Peter's unusual musical talent.

The present composition is a solo for a Soprano with strings and presumably organ. The structure is simple, but the melodic lines are charming, and the harmonic setting well made. The instruments open the piece in B flat maj. with an interlude of 8 measures. The larger part of it is used for the first period of the vocal section, which modulates toward the dominant. An interlude of 2 measures reaffirms the cadence. The second period of the vocal section starts like the first one, a fourth lower, and modulates to the related minor. The section in triple time is kept throughout in E fl. maj.

The composition is reproduced in this Catalogue, Plates F, G, H and included in the first volume of Music of the American Moravians, published by The New York Public Library.

MANUSCRIPT. Score p. 2 and 3. Systems of 5 staves, including Vlo I, Vlo II, Vla, S, B (without figures).

2. Zum 29n Aug. 1770.

ER ERQUICKET MEINE SEELE P.

Angenehm und munter 2/2, 62 meas. Prel. 15, interl. 7, postl.
3 meas. C maj.

Peter continued his composing with a Duetto for 2 Sopranos.
Less attractve and stiffer than the preceding Solo, this Duetto
proves that Peter was still a beginner. The vocal parts sing in
parallels, mostly thirds, nearly the entire piece. Peter's interest
in instrumental compositions which is made evident by a pile of
copies which he made from 1767 to 1770, becomes apparent by
the importance given to the instruments in his first compositions.
Here, nearly half the 62 measures are purely instrumental. The
prelude is in its first half repeated at the beginning of the vocal
section; the beginning of the second period is not used at all
afterwards, while the continuation uses freely the beginning of
the first theme. After a full cadence in the dominant in meas. 29,
new material is introduced, the nine measures of this middle
section being the finest part of the composition. The interlude
recapitulates the beginning of the prelude first in the dominant,
then in a modulation which leads back to the tonic in which the
voices enter with another recapitulation of the theme. The very
fine short postlude deserves special mention.

MANUSCRIPT. Score p. 4-8. Systems of 5 staves as in the
preceding pieces, the solo parts being written on the same staff.

3. Zum 29t Aug. 1772.

1.) ES IST EIN KÖSTLICH DING, DASS DAS HERZ VEST WERDE, WELCHES GESCHIEHET DURCH GNADE.

Duetto andante 3/4, 52 meas. Prel. 10, interl. 2, postl. 5 meas.
E fl. maj.

This Duetto which was written two years after the preceding
one, while Peter was still at Nazareth, may be called Peter's first
full proof composition. It excels most of Peter's early compositions and surpasses all specimens of its type written by American Moravians. Its dominant feature is the "Lombardian" combination of a 16th with a slurred dotted 8th note. The melodic
line is unusually fine, the harmonic setting properly chosen. The
voices are more independent from each other than in the preceding composition. After the prelude, the second soprano enters
alone, starting as the instruments started before. Then the first
soprano answers in the dominant. The voices enter together over
a pedal point of the dominant.

Parts to this composition appear in a series of 7 pieces written by Nitschmann. The first pieces in this series which is typical for the manuscripts of this time are composed by Gregor, the fourth being the present Duetto. The author of the fifth is not known. The sixth is Dencke's *In allen Dingen lasset uns,* the seventh Peter's *O Chor des HErrn* which is commented upon below, under No. 4. These parts presumably were used for Bethlehem shortly after Peter composed the pieces.

MANUSCRIPTS.

BETHLEHEM.

Score p. 9-11. Systems of 6 staves, Vlo I, Vlo II, Vla, S I, S II, B.

Parts. Holograph — C pr. oct. *z.29. Aug. 1772,* possibly belonging to Peter's original set. C sec., Vlo I/II, Vla, B Ob, oct., probably copied later. Org. fol. It is hard to say when this part was written. Probably it did not belong to I N's set, but was supplied to it not much later.

I N parts — see description of Dencke's *In allen Dingen;* TILL — add. C pr.

LITITZ. H W — C pr., C sec., Vlo I/II, Vla, Vlc., org.

4. Zum 29t Aug. 1772.

2.) O CHOR DES HERRN, DER VATER, DER DICH LIEB-ET, DER SEGNE UND BEHÜTE DICH STETS DURCH SEINE GÜTE P.

Andante 2/4, 12. meas. Adagio 3/4, 6 meas. G maj. *Dieses wird 3 mal wiederholt.*

This composition, which was intended for the same festival as the preceding Duet, shows that Peter did not dare to give his chorus any intricate material to perform. The composition consists of a solo for Soprano, and a choral ritornello. The second half of the adagio is in the third verse sung by the congregation. The sections are well fitted together in this simple composition, which is a fine example of this early style of alternating service.

The piece ends the series compiled by Nitschmann which is mentioned in the commentary on the preceding Duet. It was apparently intended for that place as it includes the Amen.

MANUSCRIPTS.

Score p. 12. Systems of 8 staves, Vlo I, Vlo II, Vla, S. S. A, B, instr. B.

Parts — see Dencke's *In allen Dingen;* H W — add. instr. B. I N heads the part sections with Andantino and *Choralmensur.*

5. Zum 10n Jan. 1773. (Zum Knabenfest 1773).

FREUET EUCH, IHR SÖHNE UND KINDER
SEINES VOLKS P.

Lebhaft 2/2, 49 meas. Prel. 11, interl . 4, postl. 10 meas. G maj.

This composition, the last one Peter wrote at Nazareth, presumably represents the first real choral composition Peter attempted to write. It is for three voices only, being unique among Peter's works in this respect. The melodic and harmonic quality of the piece is not more than fair, but lively instrumental parts make the composition attractive.

MANUSCRIPTS.

Score p. 13-15. Systems of 7 staves, Vlo I, Vlo II, Vla, S, A, B, instr. B.

Holograph parts — No. 52.2 written *d. 12n Dec. 1776.* The title on the organ part reads : *Zum 12n Jan. 1777 à Due Violini, Viola, Canto 1 & 2. e Basso, Basso e Organo.* The comp. is preceeded by one of Gregor, for the same combination of voices and instruments. C pr., C sec., CB, Vlo I/II, Vla, B. Of the org. only the first two pages, including the title and the part to Gregor's piece are preserved. The latter confirms that Peter used, already then, an organ reduction, not a figured bass only as organ part. Whether he actually played this during the performance, or used it as basis for a free harmonic accompaniment only we do not know. The fact that Peter often supplied his organ reductions with figures. makes probable that he used the reductions for rehearsals, and as a background for the actual continuo he was going to play.

6. Zum 6t Jun. 1773.
DOXOLOGIE ZUR ACOLUTHIE ANNAHME
HERR UNSER GOTT, DU HAST DIESE BRÜDER
UND SCHWESTERN P.

Presumably Peter's first composition for a 4 part chorus. It is a liturgy in the strictest sense. No interludes are given, and the setting is nearly throughout kept note against note. The composition is well written lacking neither melodie attractiveness nor expression, in spite of the restricted possibilities of the style. Peter wrote the piece after he returned to Bethlehem.

MANUSCRIPT. Score p. 16-18. Systems of 4 staves, S, S, A, B. On top a remark *Instrumenti colle voci.*

7. Zum 29th Aug. 1773.
EIN JEGLICHER SEY GESINNET, WIE JESUS
CHRISTUS AUCH WAR.

Andante 2/4, 24 meas. Prel. 7, postl. 5 meas. B fl. maj.

Another Duet for 2 Soprani, short and of less interest than the preceding Duets (see Nos. 2 and 3.). The setting of the prelude is used for the beginning of the vocal section and the postlude, the second phrase of the vocal section referring to the beginning of the instrumental parts.

MANUSCRIPT. Score p. 19-20. Systems of 6 staves as in No. 3.

No. 40.

Partitur

zum 4n May 1774.

Due Violini, Viola, Canto I & II do, Alto, Canto Basso & Fondamento.

1.

FREUET EUCH GOTTES, EURES HEILANDES P.

Moderato C, 48 meas., Langsam 3/2, 24 meas. a min. Prel. 10, 4 interl. 2, postl. 9 in C, postl. 5 in 3/2 section.

Peter's oldest concerted composition for chorus in 4 parts known. In the first section the instruments are quite independent and lively. The prelude recalls strongly the instrumental music Peter copied while at school in Germany. The second section uses the instruments to reinforce the voices: *Instrumenti col Canti* (Sic!). The setting approaches that of a chorale, except for the postlude.

2.

EUER LEBEN IST VERBORGEN MIT CHRISTO IN GOTT P.

Andante 2/2, 24 meas. Ein wenig munterer 20 meas. Adagio 4/2 (Alla breve), 17 meas. D maj. Prel. of 11, postl. of 3 in first section, postl. 10 in second section, 2 interl. of 2 and postl. of 4 in last section.

As in the previous composition, a combination of styles is used. The first two sections use the same type of material, although the second is melodically independent. The third section uses the style of the chorale, with interludes. It would seem that Peter never used this form again. Apparently he felt that if he wanted to introduce chorales they should be traditional hymns and plainly sung.

The second Soprano enters 4 meas. after the other voices. Possibly the pieces were performed by single singers, the second Soprano not being very good.

MANUSCRIPT. Holograph score — 8 pages incl. title page. Dated *d. 14n Febr. 1775.* Peter must generally have written his compositions first in parts, and scored only later on, if he did it at all. The systems of the score include 8 staves, Vlo I, Vlo II, Vla, S, S, A, B, instr. B.

No. 42.
Partitur
einer Music zum 4ten May 1775.

1.
DAS LAND IST VOLL ERKENNTNISS DES HERRN P.

Munter 2/2, 38 meas. Prel. 5, 2 interl. 2, postl. 2 meas. B fl. maj.

Short, but regular anthem. In the vocal sections the instruments go in unison with the voices. The instrumental phrases are rather short as in most of Peter's early works. The entrances of the voices are made with imitations, a rare feature in the compositions of the Moravians.

2.
BLEIBET IN MIR UND ICH IN EUCH P.

Andante, 21 meas. Prel. 7, interl. 1, postl. 2. G maj.

We may call this piece an Aria for chorus. No words are repeated after those of the first line which are sung twice. The setting is that of note against note, the instruments joining the voices.

MANUSCRIPTS. Holograph score — 6 pages, including title page. Systems of 8 staves, Vlo I, Vlo II, Vla, S I, S II, A, B, instr. B.

No. 43.
Partitur
Der Musicalichen Losung Zum 29ten August 1775.
à Due Violini, Viola, Canto I & II, Alto, Canto Basso,
Basso è Organo.
GOTT DER HERR IST MEINE STÄRKE UND MEIN PSALM, UND IST MEIN HEIL.

Gravitaetisch u. lebhaft 2/2, 53 meas. Prel. 11, interl. 4, 8 and 3, postl. 2 meas. D maj.

The instruments are handled quite brilliantly in this score. The choral parts are kept in a simple style, mostly note against note. The beginning of the vocal section, with effective rests is used three times.

Parts to this composition are handed down in a series which is typical for the combinations used in the first decades of Bethlehem church music.

No. 1. *Choral. Nun lob ein Seel den HErren.*

No. 2. *vide Music di Geisler zum Schluss des Jahres 1762.*

No. 3. *Losung* . . . (the present piece)

No. 4. *Accompagnement* (solo) *So spricht der HERR: Dis Volk habe ich mir selbst zugerichtet p. di Gregor.*

No. 5. *Chorus. Wie köstlich sind vor uns, Gott, Deine Gedanken p. di Gregor.*

No. 6. *Nun der Gott des Friedens heilige euch durch und durch p. di Gregor.*

The parts to Nos. 1-3 and the vocal parts to No. 6 are written by Peter, the other parts by Nitschmann. The organ part to all the 6 pieces, including chorales sung by the congregation, was made by Peter. The violin parts include after No. 5, in Peter's handwriting, parts to *Heiliget den HErrn Zebaoth* (see No. 59) with the remark:

Statt No. 3. Grave con expressione. Los. (ung) den 29t Aug. 1777. Presumably the original set of parts (at least the Nos. 1-3), used on Aug. 29, 1775.

MANUSCRIPTS.

Score, holograph — 4 pages, including title page. Systems of 8 staves, according to the title.

Parts. Holograph — C pr., C sec., A, Vlo I/II, Vla, B, org. fol.; I N — add. C B, with signature, crossed out later and replaced by the remark: *Led(ige)Schw(ester)n.*

No. 44.

Partitur

Der musicalischen Losung

ER WIRD DIR GNÄDIG SEYN, WENN DU RUFEST P.

zum Witwer- und Witwen-Fest d. 31ten Aug. 1775.

à Due Violini, Viola, IV Canti, Basso & Organo.

Affectuoso 3/8, 77 meas. Prel. 14, interl. twice 4, postl. 9 meas. B fl. maj.

A regular size anthem. The prelude is well kept together and seems to develop a longer line than most of Peter's early compositions. The choral parts are handled more freely than in the preceding works. Both the higher and the lower parts are occasionally introduced without the others.

Peter included in this score also the piece which is reproduced in facsimile opposite the title page of the present catalogue. It is called:

Ein apartes Stück aufs Clavier

ICH WILL VOR DEM HERRN SPIELEN, DER MICH
ERWÄHLET HAT.

SINGT IHR SÄNGER, SPIELT IHR REIGEN, TÖNT ZU-
SAMMEN, SPIELT UND TÖNET WIEDER SCHÖN.

Moderato 2/4, 15 meas. D maj.

This composition is unique among Peter's works. It is a song
for a Soprano with accompaniment of a harpsichord, clavichord
or piano forte. It would seem that Peter has written the text,
which is rhythmical but not rhymed, himself. The song may
have been composed for one of the informal meetings of the
Collegium musicum.

MANUSCRIPT. Holograph score — 8 p. The anthem is written on p. 3-6, the song on p. 7.

No. 59.

Partitur

Der Musicalischen Losung zum 29t Aug. 1777.

HEILIGET DEN HERRN ZEBAOTH. DEN LASSET EURE
FURCHT UND SCHRECKEN.

con due Corni, Due Violini, Viola, Violoncello è Organo.

Grave con Expressione 3/4, 58 meas. At meas. 33 the indication Geschwinder. Prel. 12, interl. twice 3, postl. 3 meas. E fl.
maj.

The striking composition is one of the best examples of Peter's
early style. In the beginning, the succession of dotted eighth
notes and triplets with sixteenth notes, and of dotted sixteenth
with thirty-seconds is quite effective. The Geschwinder starts with
a series of suspensions in the top voices against an instrumental
bass with dotted eighths and sixteenth; here we find the most
outspoken remembrance of patterns of the first half of the 18th
century.

MANUSCRIPTS.

Holograph — Score 4 p. The Co. are written on the first and
last page, added apparently after the score was written, but
before the title was put in.

Parts. Following *Make a joyful noise unto the Lord, composed
for the anniversary of the Brethren's Congregation at Bristol in
1808 by J. C. Latrobe,* one of Latrobe's finest compositions. 2 S I,
2 C pr. II, C sec. II, A I/II, T I B I, — Co. I/II in E fl., org.
8vo, Vlo I/II, Vla, Vlc.; Vlo I/II see also *Gott der Herr,* before 1777.

No. 90.

Liturgie zu Trauungen.

HERR, HERR GOTT, DER DU SELBST DIE EHE GESTIFTET UND GESEGNET HAST.

A composition which certainly belongs to the finest examples of this monotonous but impressive style. It is reproduced in facsimile at the end of this catalogue, Plates B and C. The liturgy is based upon one by Gregor and Francke.

MANUSCRIPT. Holograph score.

Peter's score No. 90, written *d.14n Jan. 1780* includes the *Liturgie 1.) bey der Acoluthen - Annahme, 2.) bey der Consecration zu Diacons u. Diaconissen, 3.) bey der Ordination eines Priesters, 4.) bey der Ordination der Bischöffe di Gregor & Franke.* This score of 12 p. is copied from a score, which included the liturgies mentioned before, as Nr. 1.) and another *Liturgie bey Trauungen,* as Nr. 2.). The latter liturgy for weddings presumably was by the same authors as the preceeding liturgies. Peter followed the original rather closely, but inserted instrumental interludes and made the melodic lines more attractive and expressive with comparatively small alterations. He copied the older score and composed his liturgy for weddings while at Lititz. The older score shows a handwriting which is found in other manuscripts from Lititz also. Probably it was transferred to Bethlehem by mistake. Peter's composition is reproduced in this catalogue, Plates F and G.

No. 102.

DER DICH GEMACHT HAT, IST DEIN MANN P.

z. 29. Aug. 1781. Choro.

Vivace Grave 2/2, 39 meas. Prel. 9, postl. 3 meas.

Peter's set of parts No. 87 includes a *Choro con due Fagotti di Joh. Ren. Verbeek* and Herbst's solo *Siehe das ist Gottes Lamm.* It was written *d. 30. May 1779.* Added on the title page is the present composition. It would seem that it was also added in the single parts. The title page indicates that the parts belong *zur Partitur 102,* which is lost. Most of the parts are unfortunately lost also. The parts make an interesting impression. As Peter left Bethlehem during September, 1779, it seems possible that he composed the present piece for the future, before he went away.

MANUSCRIPT. Holograph parts — Vlo I, instr. B and org. only. oct.

Nos. 145 and 149.
(No. 146.147.148 s. apart — without indication of title)
No. 145. Zum 13n Nov. 1786.
1.) DER HERR IST IN SEINEM HEILIGEN TEMPEL P.
Solo

2/4, 49 meas. Prel. 6, interl. 5.4 and 2, postl. 4 meas. E fl. maj.
One of the rare soli of Peter's, and among these the most striking. The composition was written at Salem, slightly more than 6 months after Peter married Catharina Leinbach, said to have been the solo soprano of the congregation. Especially detailed dynamic marks indicate the care with which Peter handled the piece which is intense and delicate. It is included in the first volume of the Music of the American Moravians. No solo has been found as yet composed by Peter at a later date.

MANUSCRIPT. Holograph score — page 1/2. Systems of 5 lines, Vlo I, Vlo II, Vla, S, instr. B.

2.) NUN BEKRÄFTIGE DEIN WORT, UNSER VATER VOLL ERBARMEN P. *Tutti.*

Lebhaft mit Nachdruck 2/2, 27 meas. Prel. 2, 3 interl. 1, postl. 1 meas. G. maj.
The choral parts of this composition are completely in the style of a chorale. The melody, not included in Gregor's tune book, might be written by Peter. The text mentions Salem in the sixth line:

> HErr bekräftige dein Wort,
> das du über diesen Ort,
> über Salem, Deine kleine
> doch erwehlte Kreuzgemeine
> über dis dein Volk und Haus
> selbst in Gnaden strahlest aus.
> Mache es zum Gottes-Haus.

MANUSCRIPT. Holograph score — p. 3/4. Systems of 7 staves, Vlo I, Vlo II, Vla, S I/II, A, B, instr. B.

No. 149. Zum Grossen Sabbath d. 7 Apr. 1787.
UNSER HERR JESUS CHRISTUS IST FÜR UNS GESTORBEN P.

Affettuoso u. fröhl. 3/4, 71 meas. Prel. 12, interl. 6, 3 and 3, postl. 6 meas. G maj.
Regular anthem, in a more concerted style than the previous composition. It deserves special attention as the only example of its type written in Salem and preserved in the Northern Province.

MANUSCRIPT. Holograph score — p. 5-8. Systems of 7 staves as in No. 145.2.

SIX QUINTETTI
à
Due Violini, Due Viole è Violoncello
di Joh. Friedr. Peter
d. 9. Jan. 1789

Quintetto I.
D major
Allegro con Brio 3/4, 45 and 78 meas.* D maj.
Andante amoroso mezza voce 2/4, 24 and 26 meas. G maj.
Allegro brillante 6/8, 54 and 77 meas. D maj.

Quintetto II.
A major
Allegretto 6/8, 51 and 81 meas. A maj.
Poco adagio 2/4, 16 and 20 meas. a min.
Presto assai 2/4, 74 and 91 meas. A maj.

Quintetto III.
G major
Presto dolce 2/2, 50 and 72 meas. G maj.
Polonoise 3/4, 16 and 28 meas. C maj.
Menuet Vivace 3/4, 16 and 32 meas. G maj.
Trio 3/4, 8 and 12 meas. g min.
Presto 2/4, 41 and 49 meas. G maj.

Quintetto IV.
C major
Vivace assai 2/2, 180 meas. C maj., with a middle section of
16 meas. in A maj.
Andantino 2/4, 17 and 26 meas. F maj.
Allegro non tanto 6/8, 51 and 88 meas. C maj.

Quintetto V.
B flat major
Allegro moderato 2/2, 66 and 88 meas. B fl. maj.
Adagio è mezzo forte 2/2, 21 and 26 meas. c min.
Allegro majore 3/4, 100 meas. B fl. maj. Minore, 79 meas. g
min. Majore Da Capo.

---

* Where two figures are given, the movement consists of two repeated sections. The number of measures does not include the repetitions.

Quintetto VI.

E flat major

Allegro maestoso 2/2, 145 meas. E fl. maj.

Andante Grazioso mezza voce 3/8, 60 meas. A fl. maj.

Prestissimo 6/8, 26 and 40 meas. E fl. maj.

The present set of Quintets, written in Salem, apparently represents the only contribution Peter has ever made toward instrumental music. While the Moravians had no objection to the use of instruments in the church, or to playing instrumental music in the Collegia musica, it would seem that most of them restrained themselves, for religious reasons, from writing secular and especially instrumental music. Peter apparently did not at first share this attitude, but took to a stricter point of view after he returned to the Northern Province.

The Quintets of Peter deserve special interest for several reasons. They are, naturally, the most freely conceived, most vivacious and most entertaining among Peter's compositions. They are the oldest known chamber music works composed in the States. And they hold their own among most of the contemporary works of the same type.

While at the Seminary at Barby, between 1767 and 1769, Peter copied a considerable number of instrumental works, including 12 Sinfonies by Abel, and 2 by J. C. F. Bach, as well as a long series of Trios, Quartets and other chamber music works by Haydn, Stamitz and others. In writing these copies, Peter apparently acquired most of his musical knowledge. The influence of the works he copied can be traced in the Quintets, which, however, have undoubtedly a personal character. The highest parts are quite florid; the players with whom Peter performed these pieces, must have been pretty well accomplished. The Violoncello part is easier, and the second Viola carefully avoids difficult passages.

The Quintets are handed down in a score and a set of parts, both in folio written by Peter himself. The score includes 39 pages, and 8 blank ones in which the staves only are drawn. The part of the Viola Prima, is unfortunately lost. The first violin is signed, on top *J. F. P. d. 28, Febr. 1789.* At that time, the score presumably was already finished. Parts and score are marked *No. 64-69.* These numbers refer to Peter's collection of instrumental pieces, later belonging to the Philharmonic Society of Bethlehem, Pa.

The entire set is included in Music of the American Moravians, No. 8.

II.

PETER'S COMPOSITIONS OF THE MIDDLE PERIOD
(Holographs in octavo with single set of vocal parts)
c. 1790- ca. 1800

No. 229.
KOMMT, LASSET UNS ANBETEN P.
à 4 Voci, 2 Violini, Viola, Violoncello è Organo di Joh. Fr. Peter

Nachdrücklich und etwas lebhaft 3/4, 61 meas. F maj.

This is a very unpretentious work of Peter's. It starts with an ascending triad as do several of his compositions. The second phrase makes interesting use of gracenotes. The prelude of 14 measures is nearly completely repeated with the chorus, after which the instruments have an interlude of 5 measures with the same material. Then the chorus introduces new material. A postlude of 10 measures starts like the second choral section, but continues with the recapitulation of the end of the prelude.

The style of the composition, the aspect of Peter's manuscript, which still, calls the lower parts CA and CB and lists the parts on the title page one above the other, confirm the early date which is suggested by the low call number. Apparently this was the first piece of Peter's composition added to the Bethlehem Church Library after his return from the Southern Province. Like the following 7 numbers, it is included in the first Bethlehem catalogue.

MANUSCRIPTS.

BETHLEHEM. Holograph parts — C pr., C sec., CA, CB, Vlo I/II, Vla, Vlc., Org.; C F S — C pr., C sec., CA, CB.

NAZARETH. Holograph parts — C pr., C sec., CA, CB, Vlo I/II, Vla, Vlc., Org.

No. 250.
DER HERR IST MEIN THEIL P.
à Canto Primo, Alto, Tenore è Basso, Flauto, Bassono,
Due Violini, Viola, Basso è Organo

di J. F. Peter

Gemeine in Bethlm 1793

Andante Vivace 3/4, 59 meas. B fl. maj.

This is the earliest composition written after Peter's return from the Southern Province which bears a date. Its form shows clearly the method Peter used in his later anthems. A prelude of 10 measures is subsequently used for the beginning of the choral part and later, first in the dominant key, and then in the tonic, for short interludes. The second section introduces slightly different material; the end of its first period is repeated to conclude the whole in a postlude of 6 measures.

The vocal parts are written simply, mostly moving in quarter-notes. The flute appears here for the first time. The violins, especially the first one, give a brilliant ornamentation which resembles very much the earlier quintets. Few later pieces have as elaborate parts for the strings.

MANUSCRIPTS. Holograph parts (instrumental parts hurriedly written) — C pr., T, CB (the original A is lost), Fl., Bassono ô Violoncello obligato, Vlo I/II, Vla., B; TILL — 2 C pr., 2 A, Organ (written out very poorly, without any regard of the instrumental parts).

No. 254.

SO SPRICHT DER HERR: SIEHE ICH VERTILGE DEINE MISSETHAT, WIE EINE WOLKE P.

Solo con Coro con Due Corni, Due Flauti, Due Violini, Viola è Violoncello è Organo

di J. Fr. Peter

1.) *Gem. in Bethlehem.*   2.) *Nazareth.*

Andante poco Adagio, Solo C, 9 meas., without Corni; Vivace, Coro, 3/4, 65 meas. F maj.

The introduction of a Solo is unusual in Peter's works, as is the title Solo con Coro, which confirms the early date indicated by the low call number. The composition is lively and well written. The solo which is intended for a Soprano may have been composed for Peter's wife. This is the first composition by Peter which requires 2 flutes and 2 horns.

MANUSCRIPTS.

BETHLEHEM. Holograph parts (A337) — C pr., C sec., CA, CB, Fl. I/II, Co. I/II (in F), Vlo I/II, Vla., Vlc., Org.

Additional parts — 3 and 1 C pr., 2 C sec., CA.

NAZARETH. Holograph parts — C pr., C sec., A, CB, Fl. I/II, Co. I/II, Vlo I/II, Vla., Vlc., Org. Presumably later than the Bethlehem set.

No. 266. Coro.
DIE GNADE UND WAHRHEIT DES HERRN WALTET ÜBER UNS P.
di Joh. Fr. Peter.
Gemeine zu Bethlehem Apr. 30. 1794.
(2 Violini, Viola, Violoncello, 4 Voci, doppelt, Organo)
Lebhaft 3/4, 74 meas. G maj.

Rather dull piece, the form of which is moulded following the usual scheme including a prelude of 14 measures, choral entrance with the same material, quotations of its beginning and ending, introduction of moderately new material during the course of the piece, and concluding postlude of 2 meas.

MANUSCRIPTS. V VL — C pr., C sec., A, B, Vlo I/II, Vla, Vlc., Org.; H W — 2 C pr., C sec., A. The instrumentation quoted above added to V VL's title by TILL.

(Original number not known)
Two Compositions

1.

ICH WILL BALD IHR HEILAND SEYN P.
Solo con Tutti & Due Violi, Viola Violoncello & Orgo
Zum Knabenfest
(di Joh. Fr. Peter. Gemeine zu Bethlm 1795)

Andante 2/4, 62 meas. G maj.

A good example of Peter's writing which reflects the sympathetic simplicity of its author. Musically remarkable are the florid instrumental parts, the use of appoggiaturas which connects *Kommt lasset uns anbeten* with the present piece, a series of diminished seventh chords (in meas. 44/45) which points forward to *Lasset uns rechtschaffen seyn,* and smaller modulations. The title *Solo con tutti* recalls the *Solo con Coro* of *So spricht der Herr* which must have been composed at about the same time. The catalogue gives the No. 54, which apparently does not represent the first call number of the manuscript.

The form is well balanced. The prelude of 13 measures is in its greater part repeated with the solo of 13 measures. The last measures of the solo lead to the dominant, with a crescendo; then the tutti comes in, and after this the rest of the prelude is repeated in the dominant key. Later, the entrance of the first solo is given by the chorus like the beginning of a recapitulation; the continuation is free. A postlude of 6 measures repeats material of the prelude, but with changes and omission of the end which had already been recapitulated.

2.

LOBE DEN HERRN, MEINE SEELE P.

Coro con Due Violi, Viola, Basso è Orgo

Zum 29t. Aug.

di Joh. Fr. Peter. Gemeine zu Bethlm 1795.

Vivace 3 (3/2) 55 meas. Etwas langsamer 2 (2/2), 34 meas. A maj.

This composition displays several peculiarities. Peter used nowhere else the French time-signatures 2 and 3, and it is hard to say where he got the idea of writing a 3 with a stroke in order to indicate the halfnotes. The organ-part is less complete than all his others; it mostly indicates but two of the upper parts, at some places only one. At another place he gives parallel octaves, certainly not by mistake, but to make the part sound fuller. The composition is of comparatively popular character, being a hymn or Arietta rather than an anthem. The importance of the instruments is correspondingly restricted. They give the melody a first audition in a prelude of 12 measures and fill out eventually the rests of the voices, but have no independent lines besides, in strict contrast to most of Peter's compositions, including the one on the back of which the parts are written and which has a rather florid instrumental accompaniment.

MANUSCRIPTS.

BETHLEHEM. Holograph parts — C pr., C sec., CA (for 1. only), CT (for 2. only, on the back of CA for 1.), CB; Vlo I/II, Vla, B, Org.

Add. — 3 C pr., 2 C sec. for 2. only.

LITITZ (2. only). H W — C pr., C sec., T, B, Vlo I/II, Vla, B, Org.; P Wolle — C pr. I/II, C sec. II.

No. 273.

NICHT UNS, HERR, SONDERN DEINEM NAMEN GIB EHRE, UM DEINE GNADE UND WAHRHEIT.

à Due Corni, Due Flauti, Due Violini, 4 Voci,

Viola, Basso è Organo obligato   di Joh. Fr. Peter

Der Gemeine zu Bethlehem verehrt vom Verfasser

Maestoso con Grave è Moto C, 72 meas. E fl. maj.

One of Peter's most carefully contrived and most striking works. It does not seem that he put the dedication mentioned above, which is found on the cover to the organ part, in himself, but the elaborate indication of the tempo and character of the piece as well as an unusual number of dynamic marks prove that Peter made a special effort to do his best in this composition.

Moreover, this is the only example of an organ part by Peter being called "Organo obligato." The first theme may be considered as the finest Peter has ever invented. The contrast of devotion and glamour is perfectly expressed throughout the piece. For which special occasion the composition may have been intended, we cannot say. Peter possibly made this contribution to the Bethlehem church music when he was at Hope, or came back from there, or most probably as a kind of masterpiece when he was made organist of the church. The date of this event, however, is not exactly related. This is the last of the compositions in octavo which is mentioned in the oldest catalogue. The organ part is reproduced, as an example of Peter's technique of elaborating organ reductions, at the end of this catalogue, Plates M, N.

MANUSCRIPTS. Holograph parts — S, A, T, CB, Vlo I/II, Vla, Vlc., Fl. traverso I/II, Co I/II in E fl., Org.; TILL — 3 S. 3 C sec., T, 2B, Clar. I/II (replacing the Fl.). Till has changed the text of the first half to *Von Gnade und Recht wollen wir singen, Herr, und Dir lobsingen p.* It is obvious that the new text does not fit the composition.

No. 411.

2 Cori

Con due Flauti è Fagotto, Due Violini, Viola è Violoncello è Organo di J. Fr. Peter

1.

LASSET UNS RECHTSCHAFFEN SEYN IN DER LIEBE, UND WACHSEN IN ALLEN STÜCKEN AN DEM, DER DAS HAUPT IST, CHRISTUS.

Munter 3/8, 119 meas. A maj.

Instrumental prelude of 30 measures. The second half of it is repeated as postlude, and partly as interlude. This is one of the best instrumental sections in Peter's vocal music; note the irregularity of the meter in the first section and the sequence of imitations between the violins, on 7th-chords which descend in fifths, in the second. It is made available as No. 2 of Music of the American Moravians, by the New York Public Library.

2.

DER HERR SEGNE EUCH JE MEHR UND MEHR, EUCH UND EURE KINDER.

Andante con affetto 2/2, 40 meas. F maj.

This composition which starts with a prelude of 12 measures and ends with a postlude of 4 is not very interesting; it starts with an ascending triad of the chorus and ends with a rather nice pedalpoint in repeated 8th-notes, going through 4 measures.

MANUSCRIPTS.

BETHLEHEM (A329). Holograph parts — Original set — C pr., C sec., A and CB, Fl. I/II, Viol. I/II, Vla, Vlc., Org.; later added parts — C pr. I, 2 C pr. II, C sec. II, A II, Fag. Also added Cho I on all vocal parts of the first set. Possibly the second piece was added at the same time as the more recent parts, as the title seems to include the basoon from the very beginning. Set CFS — C sec. and A to 1. only.

LITITZ. C pr., C sec., A, B, Vlo I/II, Vla, Vlc., Fl. I/II, Fag., Org. C pr. II, C sec. II, A II, B II to 1.; add. C pr., C sec. to 2. only.

NAZARETH (1. only). BECHLER — C pr., C sec., A, B, Fl. I/II, Vlo I/II, Vla, Vlc., Org.; add. C pr., A.

No. 560.

DIE MIT THRÄNEN SÄEN, WERDEN MIT FREUDEN ERNDTEN P.

Coro con Flauto è Fagotto

Due Violi, Viola, Violoncello è Organo

di J. Fr. Peter.

Andante 2/4, 68 meas. A min.

One of Peter's most inspired and effective compositions.

The beginning uses amply chromatic progressions; the contrasting *mit Freuden* is expressed with a tremolo pedal point and then with 16th-triplets in the violins. The prelude of 9 meas. is used as an interlude and shortened as a postlude; the fine ending is omitted in the interlude and thus spared for the end of the whole. The composition appears as No. 3 of the Music of the American Moravians, made available by the New York Public Library.

The number of the catalogue is apparently not the original one. The original set of parts is written on the same paper as the original set of parts to *Lasset uns rechtschaffen sein p.* and must have been written at the same time as Peter did not use this paper very long. The bassoon part is written on paper different from that of the other parts. It was evidently added later. The indication è Fagotto on the title page was also added afterwards.

MANUSCRIPTS. Holograph parts (A336) — C pr., C sec., A, B, Fl., Fag., Vlo I/II, Vla, Vlc., Org.; add. parts — 4 C pr., 2 C sec., A.

III.

PETER'S LATER COMPOSITIONS

ca. 1800-1813

A.

LARGER FORMS

(Holographs in folio)

No. 326.

MAKE A JOYFUL NOISE UNTO GOD, ALL YE LANDS P.

à Due Trombe ô Corni, Due Violini, Viola è Basso,
Due Soprani, Alto & Canto Basso è Organo
di Joh. Friedrich Peter

Vivace 2/2, 36 meas. Andante adagio 2/4, 22 meas. Tempo I, 17 meas. D maj.

One of the rare compositions in which a contrasting middle section is inserted. Here the middle section stands in the related minor key, and is more original and more expressive than the rest. The first part and the third, which gives a free recapitulation of the first, are interesting only in melodic details, the harmony being rather commonplace throughout. The composition is typical for the style of Peter's "folio" compositions, especially of those with trumpets, which, in general, display a somewhat superficial brilliancy. Within the group of folios the present work is evidently the first, as it is the only one mentioned in the oldest catalogue. The aspect of the paper, the isolated indication Trombe o Corni, and the call number affirm the above statement.

MANUSCRIPTS. Holograph parts — Org. fol., Tr. o Co I/II in D, oct. All the other parts are missing.

No. 370.

Zwey Stücke . . . di J. Fr. Peter

1.

KINDLEIN, BLEIBET BEY IHM, DASS IHR NICHT ZU SCHANDEN WERDET VOR IHM P.

Duetto con Due Flauti, Due Violi, Viola, Violoncello, Fagotto,
& Orgo

Mezzo Allegretto 2/2, 99 meas. F maj.

Apparently the only Duetto Peter composed in his later years (compare the notes on the scores 1770-1780). The rather extended composition displays good details but does not exceed the value of Peter's average compositions.

2.

DA WERDET IHR SINGEN WIE ZUR NACHT EINES HEILIGEN FESTES, WIE AN EINEM HEILIGEN ABEND P.

à Due Cori con due Corni, Due Clarinetti, Due Flauti, Fagotto, Due Violi, Viola, Violoncello & Orgo.

Lebhaft 3/4, 83 meas. E fl. maj.

The first of two compositions by Peter for an actual double chorus. The present example of this style makes a more modern impression than the other, *Lobet den Herrn* which was composed in 1801, but it is by far less striking as the setting of the choral parts is less monumental and that of the instrumental parts less independent. The text could, as Peter himself indicated, also be sung "Froh lasset uns singen" or, as Till and Schaaff indicated "Kommt lasset uns singen." The strange German used in the text makes it probable that Peter himself wrote the words.

MANUSCRIPTS.

BETHLEHEM. Holograph parts — C pr. I, C sec. I to 1., A I to 2., T I, CB I, Vlo I/II, Vla, Vlc., Fl. I/II, Fag., Org. fol., C pr. II, C sec. II, A II, CB II, Clar. I/II in B fl., Co I/II in E fl. oct.; C F S — 2 C pr. II and C sec. II; TILL — 3 C pr. I and A II, put into violin clef.

LITITZ. HERBST — S, A I, T, B I, C pr. II, C sec. II, A II. B II, Vlo I/II, Vla, Vlc., C sec. II; add. S and C sec. One of B II, Vlo I/II, Vla, Vlc.; add. S and C sec. One of Herbst's few copies of compositions by Peter. (2. only: *Kommt, lasset uns singen*). TILL — C pr. I, A I, T I, B I, C pr. II, C I/II; Fl. I by Grider, Clar. I by Bechler, C pr. II and title page by P. Wolle. Add. Contra Basso.

NAZARETH. Holograph parts — Fl. I/II, Clar. I/II, Co. I/II, Vlo I/II, Vla, Vlc. The vocal and Org. parts missing. Oct. All add. parts later.

No. 371.

SINGET IHR HIMMEL, FROHLOCKET AUF ERDEN P.

No detailed title*. The orchestra includes: Due Clarini (trumpets), due Corni, due Flauti, Due Clarinetti, due Fagotti, due Violini, Viola, Violoncello and Organo.

Allegro 3/4, 129 meas. After 59 meas. Andante, 19 meas., then Allegro. B fl. maj.

---

* Peter must have had the intention to write another chorus on the back of the sheets he used for this composition, and postponed to fill in the complete title he usually wrote until he could do that for both pieces. But obviously he never again had an opportunity to use as large an orchestra; this might be considered as the reason why he never added a pendant to the present composition.

This composition is reproduced as No. 4 in Music of the American Moravians.

Singet ihr Himmel represents Peter's most striking attempt to create monumental music. For this special occasion he could dispose about as large a group of players as he ever had. He presents them in an extended prelude with soli for the brass instruments.

The middle section introduces a Solo-soprano with obligato organ, and then a soprano duet. The organ part is carefully marked in this section. We find the indications: *Mit der Gambe allein zu spielen (nebst Flöten-Register), Bourdon allein* for the *Duo,* then *Stärkere Register.* Peter also differentiates *Choir-Manual* and *Pedal.* A note later on points out that a solo by the Clarinets could be played by the organ *in Ermangelung der Clarinetten die kleinen Noten.*

The indications of organ registers make probable that the composition was written for the inauguration of an organ. Tanneberger built an organ for Nazareth in 1793, but at that time the instruments requested were scarcely available. Tanneberger set up another organ in Salem, 1799, and it is quite possible that the composition was written for this occasion. If this be true, the indications of organ registers would be the more justified as Peter did not play the organ himself. The composition appears in an ode for Christmas 1801, presumably printed here. This would confirm the conjecture made above.

In the present composition Peter uses for the first time a double chorus in the manner which is characteristic of his later works. The chorus, while seemingly doubled, is written in 4 parts throughout. The first Sopranos as well as the Altos of both choirs sing together in unison. The Tenor is set in parallel octaves to the second Soprano; the first appears in the first choir only, while the second is assigned to the second. Who may have invented this method which was also used by Herbst we cannot say; it might go back to a tradition from Herrnhut. Here as in other cases, only a single Bass is used, in the first choir.

MANUSCRIPTS.

BETHLEHEM (A331). Holograph parts — 2 Soprano (including the solo), 2 C pr. II, C sec. II, A I/II, T I, B I; Fl. I/II, Clar. I/II, Fag. I/II, Clarino I/II (in B fl.), Co. I/II (in B fl.), Vlo I/II, Vla, Vlc., Org. Various add. parts from later periods.

LITITZ. H W — S, A, T, B, Fl. I/II, Fag. I/II, Clarin. II, Clarino I/II, Co. I/II, Vlo I/II, Vla, Vlc., Org.; 2 S II, 2 A II, B, later S II, in various hands; later Clarino in E flat for replacing Clarino in B fl., and Trombone replacing Co. I.

NAZARETH. Holograph parts — A, T, B, Fl. I/II, Clar. I/II, Fag. I/II, Clarino I/II, Co. I/II, Vla, Vlc. S and Org. missing; add. parts, including Org., later. On the back Peter's *anbetung Dir,* in Bechler's hand.

No. 372.
2 Cori

No detailed title as the organ part is lost. The orchestra includes: Due Corni, due Flauti, due Violini, Viola, Violoncello
and Organo.

1.
THE WORD WAS MADE FLESH AND DWELT
AMONG US P.

Vivace 3/4, 85 meas. D maj.

One of Peter's poorest compositions, with cheap attempts at
brilliancy. The Tenor-part here follows the Alto in its major part
without being identical with it. Apparently Peter tried to find a
solution different from that of parallel octaves which he applies
in most compositions with double chorus.

2.
HERR, DEINE RECHTE HAND THUT GROSSE
WUNDER P.

Vivace 2/2, 31 meas., Moderato 27 meas. D maj.

Slightly better than the preceding piece. The Vivace is kept
nearly throughout in dotted 8th and 16th notes of the instruments. No connection between the two sections is attempted.

MANUSCRIPTS. (A340). Holograph parts — C pr. I/II, C
sec. I/II, A I to 2., A II, T I to 1., B I/II, Fl. I/II, Co. I/II (in
D), Vlo I/II, Vla, Vlc. The organ-parts are missing. TILL —
org. Add. — 3 C pr. to 2.

No. 377.
Zwey musikalische Texte
*beyde Stücke con due Corni, Due Flauti, Fagotto, Due Violini,
Viola & Violoncello è Organo di Joh. Fr. Peter*

1. Coro
UNTO US A CHILD IS BORN; UNTO US A SON
IS GIVEN P.

Andante Vivace (sic!) 2/2, 55 meas. G maj.

In this composition, the vocal and instrumental parts are unusually differentiated. The vocal parts are characterized by the
repetition of tones with several syllables, preferably in 8th-notes,
very possibly in remembrance of themes of Handel. The instrumental parts are kept in shorter rhythms using 16th-triplets and
dotted 16th with 32nds, both rare in Peter's compositions.

The prelude of 13 measures is nearly completely repeated with the voices added; the recapitulation starts with its first phrase both instrumentally and with the chorus joining the instruments. The end is given to a cadence of the organ alone "tasto solo."

Peter's score of Herbst's *Unser keiner lebt ihm selber* presents, on the last page, a score of the wind instrument parts to this composition. It is rather hastily written; as it includes some corrections we may consider it as a first sketch. Peter must have written the other parts earlier as the bassoon part is at some places left out as being *col Violonco.* The title reads *Zu No 103 Uns ist ein Kind geboren.* The lines include Flauti (an original *Clar.* is written over, as an original *Fl* for the second staff), Corni in G and Fago. The score has 5 systems, including 49 measures; the rest is written in a single line underneath for first the flutes and then the horns, and another half line for the bassoon on the bottom of the page.

This, apparently the only sketch by Peter which is preserved, is quite interesting. Peter obviously was not used to sketch in score; he probably wrote the organ-part of his compositions first and wrote the parts out after that. The present composition probably was first conceived with an accompaniment of strings and organ only. The parts for the wind-instruments are, at places, different from the version finally adopted.

It is remarkable that Peter uses the German title as the composition itself used the English words. We may assume that Peter first composed the piece with German words, for chorus, strings and organ, that he sketched then the wind-instruments, and that he gave the final version to the wind-instruments in the copy with English words. As a composition by Peter with the German words appears in the Salem catalogue it is quite possible that Peter composed that earlier version there. The English version probably was written together with the following composition. It is included as No. 5 in the Music of the American Moravians.

2. *à Due Cori*

LOBET DEN HERRN; DENN UNSERN GOTT LOBEN, DAS IST EIN KÖSTLICH DING; SOLCH LOB IST LIEBLICH UND SCHÖN.

Lebhaft 3/2, 70 meas. C maj.

This is the second composition by Peter which is actually written for 2 choruses (See above No. 370.2 Da werdet ihr singen p.). In its old-fashioned measure, and its clever antiphonal use of the choruses, the piece is quite impressive. It is reproduced as No. 6 in Music of the American Moravians.

MANUSCRIPTS (A330). Holograph parts — 2 C pr. I, C sec. I, A I, B I, 2 C pr. II, C sec. II, A II, B II, Fl. I/II, Fag. Co. I/II (in G for 1.), in C for 2.)), Vlo I/II, Vla, Vlc., Org. The Co. in oct. Add. — C sec (for 1.).

No. 389.
2 Cori

No original title. The orchestra includes 2 Fl., 2 Fag., 2 Co. (2. only), strings, organ.

1.
JESU DU, O HERZE OHNE GLEICHEN P.

Andante 2/4, 113 meas. B fl. maj.

This composition, which, in several parts, is called Aria, might be based on a melody which is not by Peter. The first three verses of the text are repeated with the same musical phrases in the dominant key, the fourth without transposition in the tonic. The seventh and eighth are likewise sung to the tune of the fifth and sixth.

The instrumental ornamentation which Peter added to this melody is unusually rich. Peter disposed over two flutes and two bassoons, which he used amply as solo instruments in short interjections. The string parts also are very elaborate, made especially lively with broken harmonies in 16th. The violoncello part only is kept simple and easy. In addition to the introduction of 10 measures, the instruments play alone or dominate in more than 30 measures. The score is quite attractive although the hymn is extremely simple.

2.
WOHNEN IN ALLER WEISHEIT.
LASSET DAS WORT CHRISTI UNTER EUCH REICHLICH

Vivace poco allegro 3/4, 102 meas. B fl. maj.

This piece offers an aspect similar to the preceding one. The melodic and formal structure is extremely simple and is possibly not an independent composition of Peter's. The instrumentation is even richer than that of the preceding piece as it includes also 2 horns, but the use made of the instruments is more restricted and less effective.

The prelude which anticipates the material of the first stanzas fills 16 measures and is followed by interludes of, in total, 23 measures. Its second period is repeated as a postlude of 9 measures.

MANUSCRIPTS. Holograph parts — 2 S I, 2 C pr. II, C sec. II, A I/II, T I (with C sec.), B I, Fl. I/II, Fag. I/II, Co. I/II

(2. only, in B fl.), Vlo I/II, Vla, Vlc., Organo for 1. only. The Org. and Co. and an add. S to 1. in oct. TILL — Org. to 1.2., C sec., B to 7., Clar. in B fl. replacing Fl. I to 1., Vlo I, Co. 2. Add. — T and Vlc. later.

No. 390.

Coro/: doppelt:/*

ANBETUNG DIR, DU HEIL DER SÜNDER P.

coll' Due Clarini, Due Corni, Due Flauti, Due Fagotti, Due Violini, Viola & Violoncello è Organo di J. Fr. Peter

Andächtig, doch etwas lebhaft 3/4, 68 meas.; Allegro Vivace 74 meas. D maj.

It is remarkable that the use of the Clarini meant a considerable curb for Peter's phantasy. This fact can hardly be explained artistically as Peter has used the horns with ease. But the compositions which use the Trumpets would seem to attempt to be brilliant and festively beyond the inborn talent of the composer. Thus they are neither convincingly monumental nor charm with those intimate traits which are found in most of Peter's more modest compositions.

The present piece starts well enough with a typical I -VI- IV-V cadence, which is immediately repeated with the chorus. This unusually decisive start, however, is not carried through. The first choral part displays some fine harmonic progressions, but from the moment, the trumpets come in for the second time, the setting is rather dull. The beginning of the chorus is *mezza voce;* it is recapitulated shortly before the middle of this part.

The second part is harmonically and melodically ordinary. The best part of it is the setting of the violins which are written throughout in an effective style which actually gives some compensation for the lacking qualities of the rest. It must be assumed that Peter was not at his ease when he wrote the music as the organ-part shows several mistakes which is rare among Peter's copies.

MANUSCRIPTS.

BETHLEHEM. Holograph parts — S I, C pr. s(ive)S I, 2 C pr. II, C sec. II, A I/II, T I, B I, Fl. I/II, Fag. I/II, Clarino I/II (in D), Co. I/II (in D), Vlo I/II, Vla, Vlc., Org. C F S — C pr., C sec. II, B; add. Vlc. and T.

NAZARTH. BECHLER (on back of Peter's parts of *Singet ihr Himmel*)—A, T, B, Fl. I/II, Fag. I/II, Clarino I/II, Co. I/II, Vlo I/II, Vla, Vlc., Org. S later.

---

* "Doppelt" indicates that a double set of parts is included in the manuscripts.

No. 401.

GOTT IST MEIN HORT, AUF DEN ICH TRAUE p.

Coro

with 2 Flutes, 2 Horns, 2 Violins, Viola, Violoncello and Organ

No original title.

Vivace moderato 2/2, 76 meas. F maj.

One of Peter's poorest compositions. The lay-out is simple, the melodic lines scarcely attractive, the figuration of the strings obvious, and of a cheap brilliancy.

MANUSCRIPTS.

BETHLEHEM. Holograph parts (together with Till's *Wir haben ein Fest des Herrn*) — 2 S I, 2 C pr. II, C sec. II, A I/II, T I, B I, Fl. I/II, Fag., Co. I/II in F, Vlo I/II, Vla, Vlc.; TILL — Org. Vlo I; C F S — T, C sec., A, Org.; later — B and Vlc.

LITITZ. H W — 2 S, 2 A, T, 2 B, Fl. II, Fag., Co. I/II, Vlo I/II, Vla, Vlc., Org.; GRIDER — Fl. I; add. — S, T and, later, 3 S.

NAZARETH. BECHLER (zum 4ten May 1812) — S, A, T, B, Fl. I/II, Fag., Co. I/II, Vlo I/II, Vla, Vlc., Org.; add. — S.

IV.

B.

SMALLER FORMS

(Holographs in octavo with double set of vocal parts)
1810 to 1813

No. 444.

BEREITET EUER HERZ, O IHR ERLÖSTEN ALLE p.

Coro with 2 Flutes, Bassoon, 2 Horns, 2 Violins, Viola,
Violoncello and Organ. No original title.

Maestoso 2/2, 37 meas., solo; Vivace assai, Coro, 112 meas. E fl. maj.

Peter has written his instrumental parts on the back of parts to a composition on the same words by C. F. Hasse, an European Moravian. The tonality and instrumentation of both pieces is the same, except for an additional bassoon in Peter's setting. Apparently Peter did not consider the earlier composition as adequate. Both compositions start with a Canto solo, the earlier going up to b″ flat, while Peter does not exceed the g″. Peter's setting, in general, is less old-fashioned, richer and more vivid. It is certainly a much more suitable piece for the celebration of

Christmas than Hasse's anthem. As the call number may originally have referred to Hasse's composition only, it is hard to say when Peter's was added to the Library of the Church.

MANUSCRIPTS.
BETHLEHEM. Holograph parts, 1. independent — 2 C pr. I/II, C sec. II, A I/II, T I, B I/II, Fl. I/II, Org.; 2. on back of the parts to Hasse's composition — Fag., Co. I/II in E fl., Vlo I/II, Vla, instr. B; C F S — C pr. II, C sec. II.

LITITZ. H W — C pr., C sec., A, B, Fl. I/II, Fag., Co. I/II, Vlo I/II, Vla, B; BECHLER — C pr., C sec., A, B, Choro II; add. — C pr. II.

No. 463.
LOB SEY DEINER HEILIGSTEN UND EHRWÜRDIGSTEN RUHE IM GRABE p.

Chor, doppelt, con Due Corni, Due Flauti, Fagotto, Due Violini, Viola, Violoncello è Organo di Joh. Fr. Peter

Grave 2/2 (4/2), 14 meas. D maj.
Simple, but highly expressive setting in four parts. The style of a hymn which is freely applied to this composition is made attractive by a rather audacious use of suspensions or appoggiaturas. The instruments add a modest ornamentation to the singing parts, but no instrumental measures are inserted before the very end.

MANUSCRIPTS. Holograph parts — 2 C pr. I/II, C sec. II, A I/II, T I, B I, Fl. I/II, Fag., Co. I/II (in D), Vlo I/II, Vla, Vlc., Org.; add. — C pr. II, B, Vla, Org.

No. 482.
THE LOVE OF GOD IS SHED ABROAD p.

Coro con Due Corni, Due Flauti, Due Violini, Viola, Violoncello è Organo di Fr. Peter

Lebhaft 6/8, 52 meas. D maj.
A very lively movement characterized by the rhythm long-short-long and descending scales in 16th. The prelude of 9 measures is repeated in its major part as interlude, while an independent short interlude is repeated as postlude.

MANUSCRIPTS (A338). Holograph parts — C pr. I/II, C sec. I/II, A I/II, CB I/II, Fl. I/II, Co. I/II (in D), Vlo I/II, Vla, Vlc., Org.; C pr., presumably from a lost set of part, possibly earlier; TILL — C pr.; add. — 2 C pr., C sec.

No. 508.

1.

FREUET EUCH UND SEYD FRÖHLICH, DIE IHR SEINEN TAG SEHET p.

Coro, doppelt,
con Due Clarini, Due Corni, Due Flauti & Fagotto, Due Violi,
Viola, Violoncello & Orgo (di Joh. Fr. Peter)

Allegro 3/4, 92 meas. D maj.

This composition is more interesting than most of Peter's compositions which introduce trumpets. Although the start is not very striking, there are excellent details in the following sections, specially an ascending modulation in meas. 23 and following, and a pedal point in meas. 41 to 47. Toward the end, the instruments are quite brilliantly used.

A group of parts to this composition were added by Peter to the manuscript of a piece by Weber. This bears the No. 122, but apparently Peter's parts were added much later. No. 504 included a composition by La Trobe written in 1808. Presumably the manuscript No. 508 was written during the same year, as a copy from the earlier parts which may go back to the beginning of the century.

2.

ICH WILL DIR EIN FREUDENOPFER THUN UND DEINEM NAMEN DANKEN, HERR! p.

Coro, doppelt,
con due Corni, Due Flauti è Fagotto, Due Violi, Viola,
Violoncello è Organo di Joh. Fr. Peter

Munter 3/4, 74 meas. E fl. maj.

This composition which gives a more restricted expression of joy is by far more original and more striking than the preceding. The theme is excellent and the mood of the beginning well kept throughout the piece. The first horn which is handled more freely than in most of Peter's works goes up to the 14th, 15th and 16th partial tone (b fl., b and c, noted pitch).

MANUSCRIPTS. Holograph parts 1. No. 122 for 1. only, on back of Weber's Christus kommt her p. — C pr., Vlo I/II, Vla, Vlc., Fl., Tromba I/II (in D), and, independent, C pr. I and C sec. I, obl., Org.; 2. No. 508 for 1. and 2. — 2 C pr. I, 2 C pr. II, C sec. I/II, A I/II, B I, Vlo I/II, Vla, Vlc., Fl. I/II, Fag., Clarino I/II (in D), Org.; Co. I/II obl.; C F S — C sec. and A.

No. 525.

DAS HEILIGTHUM IST AUFGETHAN p.

Coro, doppelt geschrieben*
con Due Flauti, Clarinetto & Fagotto solo, Due Violini, Viola,
Violoncello è Orgo di J. Fr. Peter

Andante con espressione 2/2, 48 meas. E fl.

One of Peter's finest and most mature compositions. Its quiet solemnity recalls Mozart's masonic music, and his Zauberflöte. Peter uses several times the augmented sixth before the dominant, and a few astonishing harmonic progressions (see meas. 12/13). The clarinet is given a solo in one measure only, the bassoon none at all; evidently Peter wanted to indicate that there is only one instrument of each type required, rather than its importance. The composition is included as No. 7 in the Music of the American Moravians.

MANUSCRIPTS (A335). Holograph parts — 2 C pr. I/II, C sec. II, A I/II, T I, B I, Fl. I/II, Clar. (in B fl.), Fag., Viol I/II, Vla, Vlc., Org.; add. — C sec., A.

No. 533.
2 Cori

1.

DU WIRST LUST HABEN AM HERRN p.

con Due Flauti, Due Violi, Viola, Violoncello & Organo
(di J. Fr. Peter)

Munter C, 50 meas. B fl. maj.

Two sections, the first of which is slightly longer, display different although similar melodic material. Evidently the composition was written at the same time as the following piece which was composed for Jan. 11, 1813. Although one of Peter's latest works, the present one does not offer much of special interest.

2.

DEINE ZEUGNISSE SIND MEIN EWIGES ERBE p.

con Due Flauti, Due Corni, Due Violi, Viola, Violoncello
& Organo di J. Fr. Peter

Allegro 2/2, 38 meas. Più allegro, 25 meas. D maj.

This composition shows even more clearly than the preceding a 2-part form with sections independent of each other. The beginning is shortly recapitulated before the entrance of the second section which has the character of a stretto. The style of

---

* The manuscript includes Bechler's Selige Gemeinde as second number. The original title is, correspondingly, *2 Cori*.

the composition which reminds one somewhat of Mozart is more attractive than that of the preceding.

MANUSCRIPTS.

BETHLEHEM (A341). Holograph parts—2 C pr. I/II, C sec. I/II, A I/II, B I, 2 Fl., 2 Co. (in D, for 2. only), Vlo I/II, Vla, Vlc., Org.; Add. — C pr., A, B. Later choral parts.

LITITZ. C F S — C pr., C sec., A, B, Vlo I/II, Fl. I/II, Vla, Vlc., Org.* Vocal parts Choro II and add. C pr. I, C pr. II in a different hand.

No. 534.

1.

JESUS, UNSER HIRT, IST TREU p.

a 2 Violini, 2 Flauti, Fagotto, Viola, Violoncello, Organo, 4 Voci in duplo di J. Fr. Peter (Till's title)

Allegretto C, 8 and twice 22 meas. G maj.; 4, twice 15 and 2 meas. D maj.

The present composition is unique among Peter's works. It is an Arietta in two parts, the second of which introduces a new melody and different tonality. Each of the parts is sung twice, thus 4 verses of the text are taken care of. Each part has an instrumental prelude, which is not repeated for the next verse, and a short postlude. The melody has a really popular touch. Possibly it was taken by Peter from another source, but more probably he invented it. The instrumental accompaniment is quite elaborate and gives excellent relief to the melody. Schaaff's organ-part is written on three staves, with a single voice in the highest line. Apparently he used the composition for his children's chorus. It might be that Peter originally wrote the charming piece this way.

2.

AMEN, AMEN, DER HERR THUE ALSO p.

(a) 2 Violini, 2 Flauti, 2 Clarini, Viola, Violoncello & Organo. 4 Voci in duplo di Joh. Fr. Peter (Till's title)

Allegretto 6/8, 24 meas. D maj.

This, the shortest among Peter's anthems, is not more than a stretto. It does not offer much of special interest although it is

---

* A letter by C. F. Schaaff, addressed to Brother (Abraham) Levering, dated Bethlehem, d. 10ten Aug. 1817, begins: "In der Meinung, dass Du in Litiz Music-Director bist, sende Dir 2 copirte Stücke, die sich im Psalm zum 29ten August befinden, u. die Ihr noch nicht hattet. Die zwey andern Stücke sind zu bekannt, als dass ich letzteres denken könnte." A postscriptum reads: "Für Copiren der 2 musical. Stücke: Singet dem HE(rrn) u. Du wirst Lust haben am HErrn u. Pappire dazu — 85 Cents." The other composition mentioned is by Rev. Verbeck. The letter made identification of Schaaff's handwriting possible.

well written. Till claims that this piece precedes the other included in the manuscript, but apparently he is mistaken, or changed the order knowingly.

MANUSCRIPTS.

BETHLEHEM. 1. and 2. Holograph parts — C pr. I/II, C sec. I (2. only), C sec. II, A I, A II (2. only), T I (1. only), B I/II, Fl. I/II, Fag. (1. only), Clarino I/II (2. only), Vlo I/II, Vla, Vlc., Org. to 1. by C F S; to 2. added by TILL; add. parts by TILL, C F S and others.

LITITZ. HERBST (No. 138.2) — S pr., S sec., T, B, Fl. I/II, Fag., Vlo I/II, Vla, Vlc., Org.; add. — 2 S I, A. One of Herbst's few copies of works by Peter.

No. 538.

AUF SEELE SCHICKE DICH p.

di Herbst, con variazioni di Fr. Peter

3/8. Sanft und langsam, 3 and 26 meas. Piu andante Sanft und hell, 26 meas. Tempo I, 26 meas. e min.; 26 meas. E maj.

A composition by Herbst, which is lost in its original version, with variations by Peter. The original apparently was an Arietta of 26 measures, sung 4 times, possibly with a prelude of 3 meas. Peter must have preserved the vocal parts pretty completely. The variations are chiefly worked out through the instruments. The part of the first violin, which gives a good idea of Peter's technique of instrumental ornamentation, is reproduced at the end of this volume, plate 00. The whole composition is quite lovely.

MANUSCRIPT. Holograph parts — C pr., CA, T, CB, Vlo I/II, Vla, Vlc., Org; C F S — 2 C pr., CA, T, CB, on same paper as Peter's parts. Add. — C pr.

No. 545.

TRÖSTE DICH ALS EINS DER KRANKEN p.

Coro, doppelt geschrieben
con Due Flauti, Due Violini, Viola, Violoncello è Organo
di J. Fr. Peter

Andantino 2/2, 33 meas.; Etwas geschwinder 2/2, 33 meas. B fl. maj.

The composition uses two verses of the hymn and is accordingly divided into contrasting sections. Peter indicates that a slightly different text could also be used: Tröstet euch, ihr Seine Kranken s. Nachtrag z(um) (Brüder) Ges(ang)B(uch) No. 272, 1.2. He added the second text with red ink, in all parts.

The present anthem, apparently as late as the original call number would seem to indicate gives an excellent idea of Peter's latest style. While rather smooth and soft in general, the composition includes a few places in which chromatic passing notes are somewhat audaciously used. The form is quite free. The prelude of 6 measures is repeated with the entrance of the chorus, but not afterwards, each of the interludes and the postlude using different material. The first section ends with the dominant chord of g minor, the second starts with the tonic of this tonality; thus the returning to B fl. major is felt like a recapitulation.

MANUSCRIPT. Holograph parts — 2 C pr. I/II, C sec. I/II, A I/II, B I, Fl. I/II, Vlo I/II, Vla, Vlc., Org. C F S — add. C pr.

No. 546.
SELIG, WER IN JESU WUNDEN SEINE GNADENWAHL ERBLICKT p.

Coro
con Due Violini, Viola, Violoncello è Organo
seinem Freunde William Boehler gewidmet am 27ten Februar 1813 von Johann Friedrich Peter

Etwas munter C, 53 meas. G maj.

Peter's latest dated composition, presumably the latest he has written. A fine piece, with harmonically interesting details. It appears as No. 8 of the Music of the American Moravians.

William Boehler was a carpenter, and served as such when the new church was built and decorated. He played the viola, and is mentioned by R. A. Grider as one of the performers who took part in the rendition of Haydn's creation, in 1811.

MANUSCRIPT (A339). Holograph parts — 2 C pr. I/II, C sec. II, A I/II, T I, B I, Vlo I/II, Vla, Vlc., Org.; add. — 2 C pr.

Appendix
DU MEINE SEELE SINGE P.

Vivace 2/2, 36 meas. Andante 2/4, 22 meas. Tempo I, 17 meas. D maj. Middle section in b min.

This composition is attributed to Peter by Till. In addition to being extremely poor, it relies on means Peter would scarcely have used. The attribution to Peter is probably wrong, but we cannot name the composer. Possibly the composition was written by Till himself, who furnished the only manuscript known.

MANUSCRIPT. TILL — 1.) S, C sec., A, B, Vlo I/II, Vla, Vlc., Org. 2.) 2 S, 3 C sec., Co. o Trombe I/II in D, presumably added later.

JACOB VAN VLECK

Jacob van Vleck, born at New York in 1751, was the first Moravian born in America who did some composing. He was the son of Henry van Vleck, a merchant, of a Dutch Reformed family, who, having been the agent of the Brethren for some time, moved to Bethlehem in 1773. Jacob studied at Nazareth and later at Barby. He returned from Europe in 1778, and became assistant pastor of the Bethlehem congregation. From 1790 to 1800, he was .inspector of the Young Ladies' Seminary. Later on he worked successively as inspector of Nazareth Hall, at Lititz and Salem. In 1815, he was consecrated a bishop, and returned to Bethlehem. He died there, July 3, 1831.

The musical activities of this brilliant man were restricted by the sum of his other activities. Only four of his compositions are preserved. Two of these are mentioned in the earliest Bethlehem catalogue, together with a *Duetto Ich freue mich in dem Herrn,* and another piece *Der dich gemacht hat,* which are lost. The quality of the compositions preserved proves that Van Vleck was a fine musician. Till asserts that van Vleck played an important part in the improvement of music at Bethlehem. Eventually he cooperated with Nitschmann, his brother-in-law, by writing out organ parts to sets of parts copied by Nitschmann.

Van Vleck is pictured in the drawing reproduced at the end of this volume, plate X.

BLUTGE LEIDEN MEINES EIN'GEN FREUNDES P.

Feierlich 2/2, 26 meas. B fl. maj.

A well written Arietta, almost entirely in the style of a chorale. It is also preserved with the English text *Bleeding, suffering, agonizing Jesus p.*

MANUSCRIPT. H W — 2 C pr., 2 C sec., 2 CA, 2 CB, Vlo I/II, Vla, B and Org., partly on the back of parts to a composition by Gambold with the same words. Add. parts by C F S and later.

GOTT SEY UNS GNÄDIG P.

Mässig 2/2, 45 meas. Prel. 5, postl. 6 meas.

Simple anthem, similar in style to a liturgy, with modestly independent instrumental parts. Mentioned in Bethlehem catalogue, but handed down in Nazareth only.

MANUSCRIPT. NAZARETH. Unknown copyist — C pr., C sec., A, B, Vlo I/II, Vla, Org. (figured bass).

RUH SANFT UND WOHL P.

Andantino 2/4, 12 meas. Choral Mensur 3/4, 6 meas. G maj. 3 verses.

The first part is sung by two canti, the second, like a ritornello, by the chorus. The composition, which is intended for a child's funeral, was written before 1791 as it exists in parts by Nitschmann. It is unpretending, but well suited for the occasion.

MANUSCRIPT. I N — A, B, Vlo I/II, Vla, B; H W — C pr. and C sec. Add. — Org. and other parts by TILL and C F S. Add. text in several of the choral parts.

SINGT IHR ERLÖSTEN, SINGT GROSS UND KLEIN P.

Allegretto 2/4, 32 meas.; 3/4, 18 meas.; 2/4, 14 meas. D maj.

The only real anthem by Van Vleck preserved, written before 1791, and mentioned in the oldest Bethlehem catalogue. Three-part form, in which a contrasting middle section is introduced, but no recapitulation.

MANUSCRIPTS. Holograph parts — C pr., C sec., A, B, Vlo I/II, Vla, Vlc.; I N — C pr., C sec., A, CB, the third section being added by TILL; H W — Fl., Co. I/II in D. Org. by TILL.

JOHN CHRISTIAN TILL

John Christian Till, baptized Johann Christian, was born at Gnadenthal, May 18, 1762. He was sent to school at Nazareth, and started playing the organ at the age of eleven, continuing for more than 70 years. He was first taught by Simon Peter (see appendix). After living a few years at Bethlehem, he went to Hope as organist and teacher, then as Hausdiener to Christianbrunn near Nazareth. In 1793, he returned to Hope and stayed there until the community, which did not succeed, was given up in 1808. He went to Bethlehem where he made furniture, and later on, with his son, pianos. After J. F. Peter's death in 1813, Till became organist of the Bethlehem congregation, serving until shortly before his death in 1844.

Till was the first among the Moravians born in America who might be called a professional musician. Undoubtedly he was talented, but as he had neither sufficient training, nor was gifted and strong enough to perfect himself, he remained a rather pitiful figure. His *Lebenslauf* gives much information, and draws a quite human picture of his life while most of the autobiographies, which were written by the Moravians to be read at their funeral, follow a definite and unchanging pattern.

Seven authentic anthems by Till are preserved. None of these is mentioned in the earliest Bethlehem catalogue. Especially the later ones are mediocre. Two more, the titles of which appear in comparatively recent catalogues, could not be located.

Till composed, in addition to his anthems, the four liturgies, No. 28, 42, 51 and 53. A manuscript by Till contains the organ parts to these and to eleven more liturgies, five of which are anonymous, five by Hüffel and one by Früauff. Holograph parts to the liturgies Nos. 51 and 53, the latter *Zum Heidenfest*, are in the Bethlehem collection, parts to No. 28, *fur Christnacht*, written by H W, in the Lititz collection. Till's liturgies are less severe in style than the older ones and often approach the style of an anthem. They include soli for a bass as well as for a soprano; choral sections in quick tempo are also found in these compositions.

BARMHERZIG UND GNÄDIG IST DER HERR P.

Affectuoso 2/2, 24 meas. Munterer, 18 meas. d min.

Comparatively early composition, partly copied by Peter, written presumably before Till left for Hope in 1786. Style similar to that of a liturgy.

MANUSCRIPTS. Holograph parts — C pr., C sec., A, B, Vlo I/II, Vla, B, and later 2 C pr., B, Org.; PETER — C pr., 2 C sec.

EHR UND DANK SEY DIR GESUNGEN P.

Allegretto 2/2, 25 meas. C maj.

Hymn without repetitions of words. Rather stiff, except the last line in which a fivefold imitation is given.

MANUSCRIPT. Holograph parts — C sec., T, B, Vlo I/II, Vla, Vlc., Org.; add. — 3 C pr., 2 C sec. and Org. by C F S.

GOTT DER HERR IST MEINE STÄRKE P.

Gravitätisch. Lebhaft, 2/2, 53 meas.

Typical example of Till's careless writing in his later years.

MANUSCRIPT. Holograph parts — 3 S, 3 A, T, B and add. A and B, Vlo I/II, Vla, B and Org.

ICH DANKE DIR EWIGLICH P.

Andante 3/4, 93 meas. B fl. maj.

One of Till's earlier compositions, with good details, but a strange mixture of patterns which belong to different styles and are introduced one after another without inner connection.

MANUSCRIPTS.

BETHLEHEM. Holograph parts — 4 C pr. (2 presumably later), C sec., 2 C sec. vel A (presumably later), T, CB, Clar. I/II in B fl., Co. I/II in B fl., Vlo I/II, Vla, Vlc., Org.; add. — Fag.

LITITZ. H W — C pr. I/II, C sec. I/II, A I/II, B I/II, Clar. I/II, Co. I/II, Vlo I/II, Vla, Vlc., Org.

SING, O DAUGHTER OF ZION P. — SINGET DEM HERRN. IHR KINDER ZIONS P.

Allegro moderato 2/2, 84(75) measures. C maj.

Two versions of the same composition. The earlier one, with English words, proves, especially in the prelude of 23 measures, that Till had a certain amount of imagination, but without the ability to make sections of different character coherent. Later on, Till shortened the prelude to 14 measures, cutting out the more unusual details, for the sake of a more levelled style which is bare of any interest.

MANUSCRIPTS (A328). ENGLISH VERSION. Holograph parts — 2 S, S pr. II, S sec. II, A, A II, T, B, Fl. I/II, Fag., Clarino I/II, Vlo I/II, Vla, Vlc., Org. No indication for Coro I. Fl. and Clarini possibly added later. Several add. parts.

GERMAN VERSION. Holograph parts — 4 S, 3 "A or C sec.", T, 2 B, Fl. I/II, Clarino I/II in C, Co. I/II in C, Trombone basso, Vlo I/II, Vla, Vlc., Org.; add. parts later.

SO SPRICHT DER HERR, DER HEILIGE IN ISRAEL, EUER MEISTER P.

Moderato 2/2, 12 meas. Allegro con spirito 3/4, 65 meas. B fl. maj.

Apparently the earliest of the compositions by Till known. Comparatively interesting. The handwriting is similar to that of his earliest copies of instrumental works, one of which is dated 1789.

MANUSCRIPT. Holograph parts — C pr., C sec., A, B, Vlo I/II, Vla, B, Org. A later Org. part by TILL is a slightly simplified copy. Add. — 3 C pr., 2 C sec., B.

WIR HABEN EIN FEST DES HERRN P.

Munter C, 80 meas. G maj.

One of Till's early compositions. The aspect of the manuscripts makes probable that Peter helped Till in working out the wind instrument parts.

MANUSCRIPTS.

BETHLEHEM. Holograph parts — C pr., C sec., A, B, Vlo I/II, Vla, Vlc., Org.; PETER — 2 S I, 2 C pr. II, C sec. II, A I/II, T I, B I, Fl. I/II, Co. I/II in G, Vlo I/II, Vla, Vlc., fol., Fl. I/II, Co. I/II, oct., apparently belonging to Till's set of parts. Several add. parts.

NAZARETH. The set of parts mentioned for Peter's *Gott ist mein Hort* includes the present composition also.

Appendix

ALLMÄCHTIGER, DICH PREISEN WIR P.

Maestoso 2/2, 12 meas. Allegro, 71 meas. D maj.

A poor composition which follows the anthem *Herr, unser Gott, sey hochgepreiset* by J. P. A. Schulz in a manuscript by Till. The influence of Schulz's composition on the present one is evident. We must assume that Till composed it, although his name is nowhere connected with it.

MANUSCRIPT. TILL's parts — 3 S, 3 A, 2 T, 2 B, Fl., Co. I/II in D, Clarino I/II in D, Vlo I/II, Vla, Vlc., Org. This set of parts includes also P. Wolle's *Der Herr ist gross*, and was used for the celebration of the Peace Treaty, 1815.

DU MEINE SEELE SINGE, WOHLAUF UND SINGE SCHÖN P. — see PETER, Appendix.

DU SIEGESHELD, DU FÜRST DES LEBENS P.

This composition is handed down in a copy by Peter, together with *Lob und Preis und Ehre dem unschuldigen Lamm*. Both are indicated as *Tutti di J. C. Till*. Till himself crossed his name out on the composition just mentioned, and named Graun as composer. The composition mentioned above is also evidently not by Till. Both were presumably arias by Graun which Till arranged as anthems.

GEORGE GODFREY MÜLLER

George Godfrey Müller, baptized Georg Gottfried, was born at Gross Hennersdorf near Herrnhut, Saxony, on May 22, 1762. He came to America in 1784. We find him first at Nazareth, then at Lititz, and in 1793 at Bethlehem. He was ordained a deacon May 9, 1790, at Lititz, and a presbyter July 25, 1819, at Bethlehem. Later on he was minister at Beersheba, Ohio. Then, from 1814 to 1817, at Philadelphia, later on at Newport, R. I. He retired to Lititz where he died on March 19, 1821. When Zeisberger, the famous scholar and missionary among the Indians, died, Müller was assisting him.

Müller must have been an excellent musician. He was well known as a violinist; at a special occasion, he was called back to Lititz from Lancaster to entertain a distinguished guest. At Lititz, where apparently he spent the major part of his first three decades in America, he was *Brüderpfleger*, and leader of the orchestra in the Brethren's House. He assisted in building up the Church Library, especially in the years 1789 to 1791. His handwriting occurs first in the early Lititz manuscript fragments mentioned before. Later on he copied, among other compositions, a series of Herbst's works.

The compositions by Müller reveal a distinct talent, of sensitive and imaginative character. Of the eight works preserved, four are mentioned in the earliest Bethlehem catalogue, and only one can be proved as being composed after 1800. A ninth. the solo *Schau Braut! Wie hängt dein Bräutigam*, is mentioned in the Bethlehem catalogue, but lost.

FAHRE FORT, UNS ZU SEGNEN P.

Grave 3/4, 24 meas. Prel. 3 meas. E fl. maj.

A charming Arietta for chorus with instruments. The fine prelude is sustained by a pedal point. This, apparently, is the oldest composition by Müller preserved. In the vocal parts we find an informative note: *Was nicht unterstrichen ist, singen die Brüder, was einfach unterstrichen ist, die Schw(est)ern u(nd) was zweifach unterstrichen ist, singen beyde Chöre.* Similar arrangements are indicated in other early Lititz and several Bethlehem manuscripts. The bass of the Sisters' choir goes down to B fl.; whether in cases like this the higher octave was sung, or the part left to instruments we cannot say.

MANUSCRIPT. LITITZ. Holograph parts — 2 C pr., 2 C sec., 2 A, 2 CB, Fl. trav. I/II, 2 Org. Of the Org. parts, the earlier is written on 2 staves. with incomplete indication of the melody, the later on 3 staves, with complete melody, exact reduction and more generous figuration. According to the title-page, the composition required two horns, the parts for which are missing.

Coro. Losung am 24ten Juny 1787.

HERR, WIE SIND DEINE WERKE SO GROSS P.

Grave 2/2, Basso solo, 8 meas. Coro. Andante 2; 2/4 adagio 1, Munter, 17 meas.

Grave 2/2, Basso solo, 11 meas. Coro. Andante 6; adagio 3; 2/4 1, Munter, 27 meas. D maj.

Müller's most interesting composition, an excellent and well balanced combination of a melodious arioso, with choral sections. The first half of the symmetrical structure is concluded by an interlude of 10, the second by one of 11 meas.

MANUSCRIPTS. Holograph parts. 1. LITITZ set — C pr., Vlo I/II, Vla, Vlc. Other parts missing. 2. BETHLEHEM set —2 A, 2 "Coro B" crossed out, with a note *Die andere Seite gilt.* The lower half of the sheets are cut off; thus only one B is complete. On the back, complete, 2 C pr., and 2 C sec., Vlo I/II, Vla, Vlc., Org.; Add. — C pr. by TILL.

Zum 13ten Jan. 1788 als am Knabenfest

IHR SEYD THEUER ERKAUFT P.

Andante allegro 6/8, 63 meas. Prel. 7, interl. 5 and 5, postl. 4 meas. F maj.

A polished composition in fluent style, less interesting than the preceding with which it was written together.

MANUSCRIPT. Holograph parts. 1. LITITZ — as above. 2. BETHLEHEM — strings and org. only. Add. — C pr. by TILL and C F S.

MEIN HEYLAND GEHT INS LEIDEN P.

Poco lento, Suave, 71 meas. Prel. 13, interl. 9, postl. 9.

Of this touching solo an organ part only, by H W, is preserved at Bethlehem. The interlude shows, in Müller's own hand, the remark *obligate Orgel or Fl(aut)o.* A reconstruction of this composition is included in the first volume of Music of the American Moravians.

O SING ALL YE REDEEM'D FROM ADAM'S FALL P.

Moderato 2/4, 171 meas. Prel. 24, interl. 10, 17 and 16, postl.
9 meas. D maj.

Müller's only composition with an English text, the most extended and apparently the latest of his anthems. The valuable work is signed *di George Godfr. Müller 1814.*

MANUSCRIPTS. LITITZ — holograph score. BETHLEHEM. C F S — 3 C pr., 2 A, T, B, 2 add. C pr., C sec., Vlo I/II, Vla I/II, Vlc., Org.; TILL — Fl. I/II, Clarino I/II in D. Later — 2 T, 2 B.

SEY GEGRÜSST, ERBLASSTES LEBEN P.

Poco adagio, sempre piano 2/4, twice 10, and 20 meas. F maj.

A charming Arietta with well contrived instrumental parts, including an obligato bassoon. Presumably written between 1800 and 1810. The Nazareth copy attributes the composition which might originally have been a solo, to Peter, Peter to NN; the latter is corrected to Godfr. Miller by Till.

MANUSCRIPTS.

BETHLEHEM. PETER — C pr., C sec., CA, CB, add. C pr., Vlo I/II, Vla, B, Fl., Bassono obligato. Several add. parts.

NAZARETH. With title by C F S — S, A, CB, 2 copies Bassono obligato, Vlo II, Vla, B, Org. According to Peter, the composition required 2 Fl.

WIE SOLL ICH DICH EMPFANGEN P.

Andante 2/2. Twice 4, then 8 meas. E fl. maj.

Another Arietta, *The first part is first performed as prelude, and the second time the Chorus joins,* with well applied dotted rhythm.

MANUSCRIPT. LITITZ, not hologr. — C pr. I/II, C sec. I/II, A I/II, B I, Vlo I/II, Vla, Vlc., Org.

WIEDERHOLTS MIT FROHEN TÖNEN P.

Aria. Lebhaft 2/4, 62 meas. G maj. Coro C, 33 meas., a min., Dal segno al fine.

Another clever combination of a solo with a choral section. Here, the choral section forms the middle part of a da capo form.

MANUSCRIPT. BETHLEHEM. H W — C pr., A, T, B, Fl. I/II, Clar. I/II, Fag., Co. I/II in C, Tromba I/II in C, Vlo I/II, Vla I/II, Vlc., Org.

JOHN HERBST

Johann Herbst (John Herbst, or as he called himself Johannes), was born July 23, 1735, at Kempten, Allgäu. Educated at Herrnhut, he learned the trade of watchmaker. In 1759 he became Hausdiener (manager) of the Brethren's house at Kleinwelka. From 1762 to 1766 he worked as teacher in England, 1767 at Kleinwelka; 1768 he was made bookkeeper for the Warden's department of the United Elders Conference. Then he took over various offices at Neu Dietendorf, latterly being preacher there. He was ordained a deacon at Barby, March 20, 1774. In 1780 he became warden in Gnadenfrei.

In 1786 Herbst was called to Lancaster, Pennsylvania, as minister, being ordained a presbyter by Bishop John de Watteville on October 15, 1786. He must have arrived in the States early in 1787. He moved as co-preacher to Lititz in 1791. He lived there for 20 years. Appointed President of the Provincial Helper's Conference in Wachovia in 1811, he was consecrated a Bishop in Lititz. He moved to Salem, North Carolina, in 1811, and died there the following year, on January 15, 1812.

Herbst was the most prolific composer among the musicians who served the Moravian Church in America. Less spontaneous and considerably more uneven in his inventions than Peter, he seems to have been more thoroughly trained. The collection from the church at Lititz which was brought to Bethlehem in the Spring, 1938, to be preserved at the fireproof Archive, includes a book of 128 pages in Herbst's handwriting, giving an *Anleitung zum Generalbassspielen besonders für Choralspieler* in 10 chapters, or 181 paragraphs. The § 181 which discusses the technique of interludes in chorales reminds one of Gregor's preface to his Choralbuch, and the entire treatise might go back to Gregor. It proves, however, that Herbst had a well founded knowledge of harmony. He used it to write a book of chorales in 4 part setting taking over Gregor's bases and including not less than 158 chorales; it is accompanied by a triple index which first lists the chorales according to occasions, then alphabetically, and finally according to the meters. This book which also was found among the Lititz manuscripts may have served for the choir as well as for the trombones.

Herbst's manuscripts which compose the major part of the collection from the Lititz Church clearly form two groups. Those of the first group are all of the same size, 7⅜ x 9⅜ inches, and most of them written on the same paper which shows as watermark a large G and the words *GAMMER PAPPIER*. Most of these manuscripts are dated, and nearly all are marked, by Herbst

himself, with a red number. The manuscripts of the second group
are slightly smaller, and written on paper of varying make. None
of these bears a date in Herbst's hand. The call-numbers are
written in black. While the manuscripts of the first group generally include a series of compositions and often do not name the
composers, there are rarely more than 2 or 3 compositions in
manuscripts of the second, and nearly all of these indicate clearly
the author. The dates in the first group range from 1761 to 1786
which proves that Herbst wrote the entire group in Europe.
Many manuscripts of the second group are marked *Der Gemeine
in Litiz gehörig;* there is no doubt that Herbst wrote all the manuscripts of this group in America.

Early in 1795, Herbst made a catalogue of the Lititz collection.
This catalogue is highly valuable for an exact chronology of
Herbst's works. In 1795, the collection included 86 of the
manuscripts with black call-numbers. From this date on at least,
the manuscripts undoubtedly were numbered and their titles
added to the catalogue as soon as they were written. But we may
also assume that Herbst numbered his manuscripts ever since he
started to build up the Lititz collection, as he had numbered his
private European collection. For the red numbers follow exactly the chronological order of the dates, and the black numbers
correspond likewise to the few dates of compositions about
which we happen to be informed. The present catalogue lists
therefore all compositions of Herbst in the order of their call-
numbers. When Herbst left Lititz, the collection included 155
numbers, of which 148 were entered in the catalogue by Herbst
himself who is the author of approximately a third of all compositions included. The catalogue was supplemented by G. G.
Müller and others. The contents of Herbst's European copies
which, as a note on the title page of the catalogue states, were
left behind by him when he went South, were then also listed in
the catalogue.

As the present catalogue is concerned with the activity of
Moravian musicians in America, the early compositions by Herbst
are only of secondary interest. They must, however, be listed
here in so far as copies of them were used in the American settlements, in order to differentiate these compositions from those
Herbst may have written in American. This catalogue starts
therefore with a chronological enumeration of those compositions
which are also handed down in copies at other places. In several
cases the attribution to Herbst is questionable as the old copies
do not indicate the author, but in general we may assume, that
Herbst himself gave his old copies to the Brethren who copied
them, mentioning whether he was the composer, or not.

The second section of this catalogue of Herbst's compositions
deals with the material written at Lititz, or at any rate, in Penn-

sylvania, either by Herbst himself or by G. G. Müller. These are listed in the order of the call-numbers of Herbst's catalogue. Several of these, however, were evidently copies of earlier manuscripts although the latter are lost. We may assume, for instance, that all compositions by Herbst which are handed down in Lititz in a copy by G. G. Müller only, were composed at an earlier date, presumably in Europe.

The third section of this catalogue of Herbst's compositions deals with compositions which are preserved at Bethlehem, but not in Lititz. All of these are more or less problematic. Not a single holograph of Herbst's was found in Bethlehem. It is obvious, on the other hand, that Herbst kept a copy of all compositions he wrote during the decades he spent at Lititz. We must conclude that the compositions preserved at Bethlehem only are either spurious or taken from manuscripts written in Europe which are lost. The latter is highly probable in many cases, especially as the numbers of Herbst's European manuscripts preserved at Lititz do by far not form a consecutive series.

The excerpts from the catalogues at Winston-Salem, which we only were able to consult, are of little help. First they do not state which items belong to the Salem Congregation collection, and which to the Salem Herbst collection, the latter apparently being one of scores only. Then they do not state whether the manuscripts of Herbst are dated, and to what group they might belong. Moreover, they include only 5 items which are handed down in Bethlehem, but not in Lititz. As these same items occur in the first Bethlehem catalogue, the probability of an European origin is considerable.

The present catalogue lists more than 100 compositions by Herbst. About 50 of these were probably written in America. The earliest Bethlehem catalogue mentions a dozen more, and the catalogue of Lancaster a few others, all of which are lost, but probably were written in Europe. The catalogues from Winston-Salem mention five pieces which are found neither in Lititz nor in Bethlehem. Whether these are preserved we do not know. As Herbst died so shortly after he assumed his office in the Southern province, it is questionable whether he did any composing in Salem. There is, however, no doubt that the systematic study of the material at Winston-Salem, which was denied to us, could furnish further information about a number of works included in this catalogue.

I.
HERBST'S EUROPEAN COMPOSITIONS
(Holographs with red numbers)

No. 90. Zum 29. Aug. 1767.
HEILIG, SELIG IST DIE FREUNDSCHAFT P.

Affettuoso 2/4, 41 meas. Etwas munterer, 49 meas. E fl. maj.
A second version of this fine composition in II, No. 102.1.
Original set — C 1, C 2, A, B, Vlo I/II, Vla, Fondamento
(Bass, not figured).

No. 96. Zum 13ten November 1767.
4.) DER HERR IST UNSER KÖNIG P.

Moderato 2/2, 63 meas. D maj.
No proof is given that this effective composition is by Herbst.
In the present manuscript, 3 out of 5 compositions included are
by Geisler. Herbst has, however, made a second version of the
piece; we may assume that he would not have done that with the
work of someone else. See II, 147.1.

Another composition included in this manuscript, *Siehe, Finsterniss
bedeckte das Erdreich p.* appears partly in a copy by Peter, as composed by Herbst. Peter was, however, certainly mistaken in calling
Herbst the author of this composition. Presumably it was written by
Geisler who wrote a setting of the same works, Lititz No. 70.2, unfortunately lost. The composition consists of two sections the first
of which only is the same in Herbst's and Peter's copy.

C 1, C 2, A, B, Vlo I/II, Vla, Vlc.

No. 97. Zum 24 Decembr. 1767.

A set of 11 numbers, 3 of which are not written out. All pieces
are of Herbst's composition.

1. *Vid. Mus. zum 24, Dec. 1765. No. 3.* Not preserved.

2. SINGET DEM HERRN EIN NEUES LIED. EIN TAG
SAGS DEM ANDERN P.

Munter 2/2, 68 meas., then shortened to 65. D maj.
Herbst copied the original version, according to a note by
G G M, *im Oct. 1790* as No. 45.1. A set of parts was made in
Bethlehem by I N, with an organ part by TILL.

3. KOMMT HERZU, LASSET UNS DEM HERRN FROH-
LOCKEN P.

Andante 2/4, 37 meas. Langsam die 8tel wie 4tel, 17 meas.
Voriges Tempo 54 meas. G maj.

Copied by Herbst as No. 57.1. A copy by I N in Bethlehem.
Set of parts in Nazareth. In Graceham catalogue.

4. *Hosianna Vid. Mus. z. 24 Dec. 65.* Not preserved.

5. *Kündlich gross Vid. Mus. z. 24 Dec. 65.* Not preserved.

6. UNS IST EIN KIND GEBOREN P.

Frölich, nicht zu geschwind, 3/4, 102 meas. A maj.

A second version is mentioned in II, No. 45.2 2 sets of parts
by I N, together with *Freuet euch und seyd fröhlich* (No. 1 of the
first and Org. of the second missing), a third one with Org. by
V VL. The same pieces in a set of parts by Joseph Schweishaupt, at Nazareth. Set of parts by TILL in Bethlehem, the horn
parts written by V VL.

7. MEINE SEELE ERHEBE DEN HERRN.

4/2, 33 meas. 3/2, 53 meas. F maj.

For two choruses. Copy by Herbst in 95.1. Two sets of parts
in Bethlehem by I N; Org. by V VL.

8. SIEHE DAS IST GOTTES LAMM P.

Langsam 2/2, 35 meas. d min.

Solo for soprano. Copy by Herbst in 19.2. Parts by Peter
dated *d. 30. May 1779* in Bethlehem. They prove that Herbst's
compositions were known here before Herbst himself came over.
Another set of parts by I N, with Org. parts by V VL, and another one; 2 add. S.

9. O DU ZU MEINEM TROST GEBORNER P.

Affettuoso 2/4, 112 meas. F maj.

Duetto for S and A. Copied by G G M *zum 24ten Dec. 1789.*

10. FREUET EUCH UND SEYD FRÖHLICH P.

Frölich, doch nicht zu geschwind 3/4, 118 meas. B fl. maj.

First composition. It was freely used in the second composition which is discussed in II, No. 148.2. Herbst copied the composition as 29.2, aided by G G M who copied the parts for the second
chorus. 2 sets of parts by I N (Vlo I of the first and Org. of both
missing), together with *Uns ist ein Kind geboren.* Set of parts
of the same composition by Joseph Schweishaupt in Nazareth.

11. UND ALSBALD WAR DA BEY DEM ENGEL DIE MENGE DER HIMMMLISCHEN HERRSCHAAREN P.

Recitativ mässig (Alto solo) 2/2, 8 meas. F maj. (Coro) 3/4,
41 meas. D maj.

The Coro is by Gregor, the Recitative which replaces the extended original prelude, apparently by Herbst.

C 1, C 2, A, B, Vlo I/II, Vla, Vlc.

(No No.) Zum gr.(ossen) Sabbath 1768.

ER HAT IN DEN TAGEN SEINES FLEISCHES P.

Largo 2/2, 28 meas. c min.

This quite expressive and well written composition is preserved with add. parts as No. 16 B, and in Bethlehem.

ER IST ERSCHIENEN, SICH SELBST GOTT ZU OPFERN P.

Andante 3/4, 74 meas. F maj.

Same parts as the previous composition.

C 1, C 2, A, B, Vlo I/II, Vla, Fondamento.

No. 109. Music Zum 4n May 1768.

1. FRIEDE SEY MIT EUCH!

Etwas langsam u. mit Affect. 2/2. 3 verses, each of which starts with a prelude. A chorale follows after each verse. 5 and 4, 3 and 3, 3 and 5 meas. In the phrygian mode.

Good composition, possibly of Herbst's. Not used later on.

2. ER KENNET DICH MIT NAMEN, UND DU HAST GNADE GEFUNDEN VER SEINEN AUGEN.

Affettuoso u. langsam 2/2, 62 meas. D maj.

Regular anthem. Used in 47.1.

The following numbers are presumably by Geisler. The text of 3. appears as 47.2 "di Geisler," and also 4. as 47.3. The text of 5. appears slightly changed as 65.1, and 6. as 22.2. all by Geisler.

C 1, C 2, A, B, Vlo I/II, Vla, Vlc.

No. 130. Losung zum 7n Sept. 1770.

(Written together with No. 126. Losung zum 7n Sept. 1769)

ICH WILL SINGEN VON DER GNADE DES HERRN EWIGLICH P.

Munter, nicht zu geschwinde 2/4, 71 meas. F maj.

One of Herbst's most attractive compositions, with a fine prelude and slight polyphonic details. Used by Herbst again in 85.1. written shortly before his catalogue, dated Jan. 5, 1795, was finished. Score by Peter, No. 199, dated 28, April 1792. Peter then was at Hope. Set of parts by I N, together with *Singet dem Herrn ein neues Lied; ein Tag sags dem andern* (see 24 Dec. 1767, 2.). Other parts by J W, V VL and Peter.

C 1, C 2, A, B, Vlo I/II, Vla, Vlc.

No. 134. Zum 29n Aug. 1771.

SO IHR BLEIBEN WERDET IN MEINER REDE, SO SEYD IHR MEINE RECHTE JÜNGER P.

Mit Affect, nicht zu langsam 3/8, 80 meas. E fl. maj.

Solo for Soprano with strings. The present copy was not written by Herbst, in contrast to the cover. Herbst used the composition later, in 107.3., which is copied by G G M. The attribution is given in the catalogue by Herbst himself.

C (on the back copied by G G M), Vlo I, Vlo II (title by Herbst), Vla, Vlc.

No. 144. Zum 17n Jun 1772.

1. SETZE MICH WIE EIN SIEGEL AUF DEIN HERZ UND WIE EIN SIEGEL AUF DEINEN ARM.

Langsam 3/4, 84 meas. a min.

The composition is attributed to Herbst in the Bethlehem catalogue only. The Bethlehem manuscript by I N is incompletely preserved, lacking the title page.

2. IHR SEYD DER TEMPEL DES LEBENDIGEN GOTTES P.

Largo 3/4, 24 meas. Andante, 27 meas. Largo, 24 meas. C maj.

The composition is attributed to Herbst by Peter who made a set of parts d. 13 Dec. 1794.

C 1, C 2, A, B, Vlo I/II, Vla, Fondamento.

No. 153. Zum grossen Sabbath 1773.

GELOBET SEY DER HERR, GROSS VON RATH UND MÄCHTIG VON THAT P.

Moderato 2/2, 55 meas. B fl. maj. 3/4, 22 meas. E fl. maj. 2/2, 6, 3/4, 17 meas. B fl. maj.

A second copy, mentioned in the catalogue as No. 44.1., was not found.

S, A, T, B, Vlo I, Vlo II, Vla, Fondamento. Add. — C 2, later, to replace the A.

No. 165. Zum 4ten May 1774

1. *Choral: Singt dem Herrn ein neues Lied p.*

2. WIE THEUER IST DEINE GÜTE, GOTT, P.

Larghetto 2/2, 30 meas. c min.

A chorus in declaiming style. A score *Zum 4ten May 1774*, in an unidentified hand, at Bethlehem. Set of vocal parts by H W.

3. DIE GEPFLANZT SIND IN DEM HAUSE DES HERRN P.

Andante 3/4, 62 meas. C maj.

Not handed down elsewhere, but possibly by Herbst.

4. GOTT ISTS, DER UNS BEVESTIGT P.

Larghetto 3/4, 77 meas. a min.

Copied by Herbst, No. 56.3.

S, A, T, B, Vlo I/II, Vla, Fondamento. No. 56. has C pr., C sec., A and B.

No. 172 Vid. Partitur. Zum grossen Sabbath 1775.

FÜRWAHR, ER TRUG UNSRE KRANKHEIT, UND LUD AUF SICH UNSRE SCHMERZEN P.

Langsam 2/2, 56 meas. E fl. maj.

One of Herbst's most expressive compositions. A set of parts written by Peter, with additional parts by Till, in Bethlehem. Set of parts as in No. 153 on the back of which they are written. Herbst transposed the composition into D maj., red No. 290. A copy of G G M in F maj. is in black No. 106.1.

No. 184. Zum 4n May 1777.

1. ICH WILL EUCH WIE EIN THAU SEYN P.

Lieblich 3/8, 64 meas. G maj.

Only copy.

2. { SIE SOLLEN / WIR WOLLEN } ÜBER SEINEM NAMEN TÄGLICH FRÖHLICH SEYN P.

Munter 2/4, 69 meas. D maj.

3. ES IST IN KEINEM ANDERN HEIL P.

Bedachtsam 3/4, 95 meas. G maj.

Copied by Herbst, No. 60.1, with C pr., C sec., A and B.

4. BLEIBET IN SEINER LIEBE, AUF DASS SEINE FREUDE IN EUCH BLEIBE P.

Angenehm 3/8, 121 meas. A maj. Duetto for 2 Sopranos.

Last number in a score, in the same handwriting as that mentioned under No. 165.2., now at Bethlehem. The first two numbers are taken from the music for May 4, 1778, otherwise lost.

Copied by Herbst, No. 56.1.

5. UNSER KEINER LEBT IHM SELBER, UNSER KEIN-
ER STIRBT IHM SELBER P.

Andante 3/4, 71 meas. D maj.
One of Herbst's best compositions, melodically and harmonic-
ally outstanding.
Copied by Herbst, No. 59. Score by Peter, a sheet of 4 pages
the last of which is filled by the wind instrument parts to Peter's
Uns ist ein Kind geboren. Peter's score indicates parts for S, A.
T, B. Set of parts by Till.
C 1, A (in S clef), T, B, Vlo I/II, Vla, Fondamento. The title
page indicates explicitly *di Herbst* being the first in which Herbst
mentions his authorship.

(No No.) Zum 4ten May 1778.

1. GELOBET SEY DER HERR, DER UNSER GEBET
NICHT VERWIRFT P.

Moderato 3/4, 75 meas. A maj.
First number of the score mentioned above, No. 184.4. Copy
by G G M, with a single part by Herbst, No. 51.2. (fol. No. 8).
Für die Gemeine in Litiz geschrieben Nov. 1790. Set of parts by
Till in Bethlehem.

2. HERZLICH LIEB HABE ICH DICH, HERR P.

Affettuoso 2/4, 63 meas. E maj.
Second number of the same score. No other manuscript
handed down.

3. SO THUT NUN FLEISS, DASS IHR VOR IHM UNBE-
FLECKT UND UNSTRÄFLICH ERFUNDEN WERDET P.

Andante 3/4, 105 meas. D maj.
Third piece in the same score, possibly written for the same
festival as the preceding anthems.
Copied by *Jer: Dencke Vor die Gem(eine) in Litiz*. No. 14,
changed to fol. 4. Herbst added *di Herbst* to the title. Vocal parts
by Herbst included, from the original set he wrote in Germany.
Single C pr. in Bethlehem.

No. 205 u. 209.

1. Zum 4n May 1779.

SO SPRICHT DER HERR ZEBAOTH: WER EUCH AN-
TASTET, DER TASTET MEINEN AUGAPFEL AN P.

Mit Affect und lieblich 2/4, 88 meas. F maj.
The C 1 starts after 6, the C 2 after 16, T and B after 42 measures.
Copied by G G M *für die Gemeine in Litiz geschrieben zum
13ten Nov. 1790,* No. 52.2.

2. Zum 29n Aug. 1779.

HÖRET ALLE, DIE IHR VOM HAUSE DES HERRN
SEYD P.

Lento 2/4, 59 meas. Munterer 3/4, 86 meas. E fl. maj.

The C 1 starts with a solo, followed by the T, and a duo of
these voices.

Copied by G G M *Für Litiz geschrieben zum 13ten Nov. 1791,*
No. 53.1. Set of parts by I N with Org. by V VL. Second set of
vocal parts by C F S.

C 1, C 2, T, B, Vlo I/II, Vla, Fondamento.

No. 255.2. Zum 24n Decembr. 1780.

HEILIGER HERRE GOTT, HEILIGER STARCKER GOTT
P. DEINER MENSCHHEIT IHR MORGENROTH.

Moderato 2/2, 27 meas. Etwas munterer, 41 meas. D maj.

First section in a style close to that of a liturgy, second section
with the character of an anthem.

C 1, C 2, A, B, Vlo I/II, Vla, Fondamento.

Copy by V VL, second set of vocal parts by H W, add. parts
by C F S.

No. 258. Zum 4n May 1781.

GESEGNET BIST DU, SEIN (MEIN) VOLK ISRAEL,
SEIN (MEIN) ERBE P.

Langsam 2/4, 64 meas. F maj.

Handed down in two sets of parts by I N, one with org. by
V VL. Herbst's name is mentioned only here. The attribution,
however, is presumably right. The composition appears in Lititz
together with red No. 257. Zum 25n Mart. 1781. *Nachdem die
Kinder Fleisch und Blut haben p.* which might also be a composition by Herbst.

C 1, C 2, T, B, Vlo I/II, Vla, Fondamento.

No. 259. Zum Begräbniss der Schw(ester) Soph. Fr. v. Seidliz
am 17n May 1781.

SO RUHE NUN IN JESU SCHOOS P.

Lento 2/4, 101 meas. a min.

A Duo for two canti with muted strings. Attribution to
Herbst in Bethlehem manuscript only. Set of parts by I N with
org. by V VL with add. parts by C F S. TILL added a second
text *O selge Ruh.*

C 1, C 2, Vlo I/II, Vla, Fondamento.

No. 261. Zum Begräbniss der sel.(igen) Schw(ester) v. Stejentin am 5n Aug. 1781.

. O SELIG BIST DU, DIE DU GEGLAUBT HAST P.

Larghetto 2/2, 35 meas. B fl. maj.

Attribution to Herbst in Bethlehem manuscripts only. Set of parts (without organ) by I N, second set of vocal parts by H W, add. parts by C F S.

C 1, C 2, A, B, Vlo I/II, Vla, Fondamento.

No. 277a. Zum 17n Aug. 1782.

O JESU, DER DU UNS VERSÜHNTEST UND UNS DIE SELIGKEIT VERDIENTEST P.

Etwas langsam 3/4, 44 meas. G maj.

Another setting of the same words, by Rolle, follows as No. 277 b. The composition is mentioned in the Bethlehem catalogues, but is not handed down there.

C 1, C 2, T, B, Vlo I/II, Vla, Fondamento.

No. 289. Zum 25n Mart. 1784.

DER HERR, DEIN GOTT, WIRD SICH ÜBER DICH FREUEN P.

Munter 2/4, 65 meas. C maj.

Copied by Herbst in double set of C 1, C 2, A, B, No. 79.2. Set of parts by H W, with add. parts by Till.

C 1, C 2, T, B, Vlo I/II, Vla, Fondamento.

No. 314. Zum 29n Aug. 1785.

SIE WERDEN TRUNKEN VON DEN REICHEN GÜTERN P.

Munter 2/4, 57 meas. C maj.

Written by Herbst on back of parts to a composition by Freydt, in an unknown handwriting. Not used later on.

C 1, C 2, T, B, Vlo I/II, Vla, Vlc.

No. 330. (No date)

EHRE SEY UNSERM HEILAND, GLORIA UND LIEBE IM GLAUBEN DEM BISCHOF UNSRER SEELEN P.

Grave 2/2, 35 meas. E fl. maj.

Simple setting, the choral parts in a style similar to that of the liturgy, the instrumental parts in dotted 8th notes throughout.

The number is written in black ink, apparently at the same time as the rest of the title, which proves that these numbers were added by Herbst before he came to America.

Copy by Herbst, for 2 choruses with A instead of T, No. 26.3., including a few add. parts. Score No. 167 with title by Peter, not written but supplemented by him; it also includes Herbst's *Lobet den Herrn, alle Seine Heerschaaren*, see No. 42.2. Set of parts by I N, C pr. missing. Another by H W, with the string parts in the original as well as a simplified version. Add. parts by C F S and Till. According to Till, the composition is a *Doxologie*. It is included in the Graceham catalogue.

C 1, C 2, T, B, Vlo I/II, Vla, Vlc.

No. 350 u. 351. 3. (No date)

LOB UND PREIS UND EHRE DEM UNSCHULDIGEN GOTTES LAMM P.

Munter 2/2, 64 meas. D maj.

The same text appears in a different setting, in red No. 121, 122, Zum 4ten May 1796, which does not seem to include works by Herbst. A third composition which is handed down in Bethlehem, is attributed to Herbst by Bleck, presumably by mistake.

Original set — S, A, T, B, Vlo I/II, Vla, Vlc. A set of vocal parts including C 1, C 2, A and B added by Herbst in Lititz. Copy of G G M with double set of vocal parts, including 2 horns in D, No. 62.1.

II.

HERBST'S COMPOSITIONS POSSIBLY OR PRESUMABLY WRITTEN IN AMERICA

(Holographs with black numbers)

No. 4.6

DAS LAMM, DAS GESCHLACHTET (ERWÜRGET) IST, IST WÜRDIG ZU NEHMEN P.

Andante mit Affect 2/2, 53 meas. D maj.

In the style of a liturgy, without considerable interludes. Possibly composed in Europe.

MANUSCRIPTS.

LITITZ. Holograph parts — C sec. I, A I, B I of a version for 2 Cori. G M M – C pr. I, C sec. I, 2 C sec. II, A II, B I/II, Vlo I of the version for 2 Cori, C pr. I/II, B II and Org. of a version for the sections of the chorus in unison.

BETHLEHEM. I N — C pr., C sec., CA, CB, Vlo I/II, Vla, B. Add. and later parts.

No. 5.
WOHL DENEN, DIE DEN HERRN FÜR IHRE STÄRKE HALTEN P.

Munter 2/2, 61 meas. Prel. 13, interl. 4, postl. 5 meas. C maj.
Regular anthem, not outstanding. Copied in Lititz from an earlier, presumably European set of parts.

MANUSCRIPTS.

LITITZ. G M M — C pr., C sec., T, B, Vlo I/II, Vla, Vlc., Org.
Holograph parts — Coro II : C pr., C sec., A, B. Add. — C pr.

BETHLEHEM. I N — C pr., C sec., T, B, Vlo I/II, Vla, B.
Add. parts by H W, C F S and later.

NAZARETH. Writer unknown — C pr., A, T, CB, Vlo I/II,
Vla, Vlc., Org. Add. — C pr.

No. 10.2. *Für Lititz geschrieben zum 24ten Dec. 1789 (G G M)*
HIER SCHLÄFT ES, O WIE SÜSS, AND LÄCHELT IN DEM SCHLAFE P.

Recitativ mit Accompagnement (mit abwechselndem Tutti und Duetto) (Peter).
Recitativo Andante C, 43 meas. Arioso 3/4, Duetto, 34 meas. and Tutti, 6 meas. D maj.
The first part is an accompanied recitative, given first to the Soprano and later on to the Basso, interrupted by the chorus to emphasize a few words, and then continued. Another short recitative is included in the Arioso. With the concluding tutti, the piece displays an excellent balance. The use of the recitative is exceptional within the music of the Moravians, the present composition being an outstanding example of it. The Lititz manuscript must be copied from an earlier one. Presumably the composition was written in Europe.

MANUSCRIPTS.

LITITZ. G G M — C pr., C sec., Org., title page, No. 10.1. only.
Holograph parts — Co. I/II, apparently a later addition. Add. — Org. The rest of the manuscript lost.

BETHLEHEM. PETER — C pr., C sec., CA, CB, Vlo I/II,
Vla, B Org. C F S — C pr., C sec., A, B, and 3 add. C pr. tutti, B tutti, Org.

No. 16(A).1.
GOTT WAR IN CHRISTO UND VERSÖHNETE DIE WELT P.

Largo 3/4, 72 meas. Prel. 7, postl. 2 meas. D maj.
Rather dull composition, probably copied from an European manuscript.

MANUSCRIPTS.

LITITZ. Unidentified writer — C pr., C sec., T, B, Vlo I/II, Vla, Vlc., Org. Holograph parts — Coro II: C pr., C sec., A, B. Add. parts — later.

BETHLEHEM. I N — C pr., C sec., A, CB, Vlo I/II, Vla, B. Unidentified — Org. Add. — V VL, H W and others. TILL — Org.

No. 18.3.
SIE FLOCHTEN IHM EINE DORNENKRONE P.

Langsam 3/4, 70 meas. Prel. 6, interl. 3, 3 and 3, postl. 3 meas. E fl. maj.

Early piece, possibly copied from a European manuscript. Good details, especially harmonically and through syncopations.

MANUSCRIPTS.

LITITZ. Holograph parts — C pr., C sec., T, B, Vla; G G M — Coro II: C pr., C sec., A, B.

BETHLEHEM. H W — C pr., C sec., A, B, Vlo I/II, Vla, B, Org. Add. parts — later.

No. 34.2. *Für Litiz geschrieben zum 13ten August 1790* (G G M) Aria. Eins bitte ich vom HErrn di Freydt. Dann 2chörig:

ZU SCHAUEN DIE SCHÖNEN GOTTESDIENSTE di Herbst

To an Aria of 50 meas., Herbst added a chorus of 38 meas., using the original postlude of 9 meas., to conclude the composition. The Lititz manuscript includes a C sec. of the original composition by Freydt. G G M copied from an earlier manuscript, possibly of European origin.

MANUSCRIPT. LITITZ. G G M — C pr. I/II, C sec. II, A I/II, B I/II, Vlo I/II, Vla, Vlc., Org.

No. 41.1. *Der Gemeine in Litiz gehörig Sept. 1790* (Note by GGM) WIR HABEN EIN FEST DES HERRN P.

Lebhaft 3/4, 81 meas. Prel. 21, interl. 6, postl. 7 meas.

This very cleverly handled work is more brilliant than most of Herbst's compositions. There is no reason why we should assume that it was not written at the time G G M indicates. Originally for two choruses, it is, in Bethlehem, handed down in a version for two choruses and two groups of strings, as a unique example of this combination. The instruments play together in the instrumental sections, but are used antiphonally in the chorus sections. Whether this version was made by Herbst himself we do not know.

MANUSCRIPTS.

LITITZ. Holograph parts — C pr. I, C sec. I, A I, C pr. II, C sec. II, A II, B II, Vlo I/II, Vla, Vlc., Org. B I missing. No second set of strings. G G M — C pr. I, C pr. II, Org. (incomplete).

BETHLEHEM. C F S — 2 S I, C sec. I, A I, B I, S II, C sec. II, A II, B II. Double set of strings, the second marked Ch. II. V VL — Org. TILL — Fl. I/II, Co. I/II (in A). Add. parts — later.

No. 42.2. Zum 13n Aug. 1787.

LOBET DEN HERRN, ALLE SEIN HEERSCHAAREN P.

Munter 3/4, 55 meas. No prel., interl. 3, postl. 2 meas. B fl. maj.

For two antiphonal choruses which are well combined. The composition was used and apparently written for the inauguration of the Church at Lititz. The date is mentioned in the score. The Ode (libretto of texts) for the inauguration of the church which is preserved in several copies, being the oldest example of its type which undoubtedly was printed and used in the Northern province, actually includes the text. Apparently, this was one of the first works, or maybe the very first work composed by Herbst in America.

MANUSCRIPTS.

LITITZ. Holograph parts — C pr. I, C sec. I, A I, B I, C pr. II, C sec. II, A II, B II, Vlo I/II, Vla, Vlc., Co. I/II (in B fl.), Org. Add. — Org. later.

BETHLEHEM. Score written in an unknown hand, but supplemented by Peter, *d. 20n Nov. 1788.* It includes compositions by Freydt, Geisler, and Herbst's *Ehre sey unserm Heiland* (see I No. 330). Parts. I N — S I, A I, T I, CB I, C pr. II, C sec. II, A II, CB II, Vlo I/II, Vla, B, Co. I/II (in B fl.). PETER — Org. V VL — Org. Add. parts by C F S and TILL.

No. 45.2.

UNS IST EIN KIND GEBOREN P.

Munter, nicht zu geschwind 3/4, 102 meas.

This is a second version of No. 97.6, written in 1765. The entire structure is preserved, but distributed among two choruses. This is the first example of alterations made by Herbst in one of his compositions. In his later years he changed several of his earlier compositions considerably.

MANUSCRIPTS. LITITZ. Holograph parts — C pr. I, C sec. I, A I, B I, C pr. II, C sec. II, A II, B II. The original string parts were used with this version. Co I/II in A added by G G M.

No. 46.2. *Der Gem. in Litiz gehörig, geschrieben im October 1790*
(G G M)

LOBSINGET DEM HERRN, DENN ER HAT SICH HERRLICH BEWEISET P.

Munter 2/2, 49 meas. Prel. 8, interl. 6, postl. 4 meas. C maj.
Ordinary anthem, with horns.

MANUSCRIPTS.

LITITZ. Holograph parts — C pr., C sec., A, B, Vlo I/II, Vla,
Vlc., Co. I/II (in C), Org. Add. parts, partly G G M — 2 C pr.,
C sec., A, B.

BETHLEHEM. I N — C pr., C sec., A, CB, Vlo I/II, Vla, B,
Co. I/II. V VL — Org. Add. parts by PETER, C F S, TILL and
later.

No. 48.2.

SINGET DEM HERRN EIN NEUES LIED, DENN DER HERR IST GROSS UND HOCH ZU LOBEN P.

Munter C, 55 meas. Prel. 11, interl. 5, postl. 5 meas. C maj.

Regular anthem, lively, but not outstanding. Herbst added 2
clarinets and 2 horns later on.

MANUSCRIPTS.

LITITZ. Holograph parts — C pr., C sec., A, B, Vlo I/II,
Vla, Vlc., Org. Clar. I/II and Co. I/II on different paper.
G G M — Coro II : C pr., C sec., A, B. Add. C pr.

BETHLEHEM. H W — C pr., C sec., A, CB, Vlo I/II, Vla, B.
Add. A. TILL — Org. Add. parts.

No. 50.2.

DANKET DEM HERRN, DENN ER IST SEHR FREUNDLICH P.

Munter 3/4, 78 meas. Prel. 9, interl. 8 meas. D maj.

Regular anthem of an early character.

MANUSCRIPTS.

LITITZ. Holograph parts — C pr., C sec., A, B, Vlo I/II,
Vla, Vlc., Co. I/II (in D), Org. G G M — Coro II : C pr., C sec.,
A, B.

BETHLEHEM. I N, first set — C pr., C sec., A, CB ; second
set — C pr., C sec., A, CB, Vlo I/II, Vla, B, Co. I/II. V VL —
Org. C F S — add. vocal parts. TILL — Fl. later instr. B.

No. 56.2.
WO EUER SCHATZ IST, DA WIRD AUCH EUER HERZ SEYN P.

Angenehm 3/4, 61 meas. Prel. 9, interl. 4, postl. 4 meas. G maj.

Duetto. Presumably taken from an earlier manuscript like 56.1 (see I. No. 184.4.) and No. 56.3. (see No. 165.4.).

MANUSCRIPT. LITITZ. Holograph parts — C pr., C sec., Vlo I/II, Vla, Vlc., Org.

No. 60.2.
SAGET UNTER DEN HEIDEN, DASS DER HERR KÖNIG SEY P.

Munter, doch nicht zu geschwind 3/8, 87 meas. Prel. 19, interl. 9, postl. 9 meas. B fl. maj.

MANUSCRIPTS. LITITZ. Holograph parts — C pr., C sec., A, B, Vlo I/II, Vla, Vlc., Org. G G M — Coro II : C pr., C sec., A, B. Add. — C pr.

No. 62.2.
BLEIBET IN MIR UND ICH IN EUCH P.

Angenehm und zärtlich 3/4, 76 meas. Prel. 12, interl. 6, postl. 8 meas. F maj.

One of Herbst's few solos. Not outstanding.

MANUSCRIPTS. LITITZ. G G M — C pr., Solo, Vlo I/II, Vla, Vlc.

No. 63.3.
GNADE UND FRIEDE SEY ÜBER EUCH P.

Moderato 3/4, 54 meas. Interl. 5, postl. 3 meas. A maj.

Mediocre anthem with good details.

MANUSCRIPTS. LITITZ. Holograph parts — C pr., C sec., A, B, Vlo I/II, Vla, Vlc.; Coro II : C pr., C sec., A, B on different paper. Org. part — later.

No. 68.2. *Geschrieben für Litiz zum 29ten Aug. 1791* (G G M)
SUCHET SEIN ANTLITZ ALLERWEGE P.

Bedachtsam 3/4, 74 meas. Prel. 9, interl. 4 and 4, postl. 5 meas. C maj.

Regular anthem with several places where the two highest voices sing alone.

The piece follows a composition by Verbeek with the same words, which gives an extended solo of the soprano as first section. Herbst's piece is by no means more striking than the older one. Probably it was Müller who put the pieces together for merely practical reasons.

No. 68.3.

DER IN EUCH ANGEFANGEN HAT DAS GUTE WERK, DER WIRDS AUCH VOLLFÜHREN P.

Lebhaft 2/4, 56 meas. Prel. 10, interl. 5, postl. 2. C maj.

Regular anthem, without unusual details.

MANUSCRIPTS.

LITITZ. G M M — C pr., C sec., A, B, Vlo I/II, Vla, Vlc., Org. The choral parts to 3 in a different hand. Add. — 2 C pr., C sec. to 3.

BETHLEHEM. I N — C pr., C sec., A, B, Vlo I/II, Vla, B. together with *Gesegnet bist du* (4. May 1781) and *Er wird dir gnädig seyn* (No. 90.2.).

No. 69.1.

DER HERR SEGNE EUCH JE MEHR UND MEHR P.

Langsam 2/2, 74 meas. Prel. 14, postl. 6 meas. E fl. maj.

Well written regular anthem, including short sections in Duo. Copied from an earlier, possibly European manuscript.

MANUSCRIPTS.

LITITZ. G G M — C pr., C sec., T, B, Vlo I/II, Vla, Vlc. Holograph parts — Coro II: C pr., C sec., A, B. Add. — C pr. and later Org.

BETHLEHEM. I N — C pr., C sec.. T, CB, Vlo I/II, Vla, B. Org. with title by Peter, probably written by him. Add. parts by Till and later.

No. 76.2.

LOBET DEN HERRN, DENN ER WIRD SEINE WAHR-HEIT TREU SICH HALTEN P.

Munter 3/4, 61 meas. Prel. 8 meas., interl. 2, postl. 3 meas. C maj.

Lively anthem without remarkable details. Herbst may have copied it from an earlier manuscript as he did the composition by Gregor with which it appears.

MANUSCRIPT. LITITZ. Holograph parts — 2 C pr., 2 C sec., 2 A, 2 B, Vlo I/II, Vla, Vlc., Org.

No. 78.1.
LASSET UNS LOBSINGEN UND MIT SÜSSEN WEISEN UNSERS GOTTES GÜTE PREISEN.

Lebhaft 3/4, 88 meas. Prel. 10, interl. 8, postl. 8 meas. C maj.

Although none of Herbst's quicker and more monumental pieces is free of commonplaces, this is a very good example of its type. The bass has more independence than usual and offers especially a vigorous figure in the postlude to the first and second half. Herbst made it considerably more striking by adding a measure in both cases. A forceful chromatic ascent is used at several places. In the second half we find twice a pedal point of 4 measures introduced by a unison. The entire piece is effective. The Bethlehem material is partly written on paper watermarked 1796, and bears a note, presumably by Till, *Gemeine zu Bethlehem 1797.*

MANUSCRIPTS.

LITITZ. Holograph parts — 2 C pr., 2 C sec., 2 A, 2 B, Vlo I/II, Vla, Vlc., Org. Add. — C pr.

BETHLEHEM. (1) C pr., C sec., A, CB, Vlo I/II, Vla, Vlc., Org.; (2) 2 C pr., C sec., A, B.

No. 78.2.
GEHE HIN MIT FRIEDEN, DER GOTT ISRAEL WIRD DIR GEBEN DEINE BITTE P.

Bedächtig 3/4, 98 meas. Prel. 12, interl. 9, postl. 9 meas. C maj.

Regular anthem of average quality. The interlude is repeated a fifth lower at the end. After the interlude a short recapitulation.

MANUSCRIPTS.

LITITZ. As 78.1. without add. C pr.

BETHLEHEM. V VL — 2 C pr., 2 C sec., 2 A, 2 B, Vlo I/II. Vla, Vlc., Org. The piece is written on the back of the parts to Herbst's *Singt ihr Erlösten.*

NAZARETH. H W — C pr., C sec., A, B, Vlo I/II, Vla, Vlc., Org.

No. 86.2.
IN ALLEN DINGEN LASSET UNS BEWEISEN ALS DIE DIENER GOTTES.

Andante 2/4, 74 meas. Prel. 17, interl. and postl. 7 meas. A maj.

The composition excels by its extended prelude which is especially fine in its last section. The interlude as well as the postlude recapitulate the last section of the prelude. The music throughout is fluent, making attractive use of syncopations and occasional suspensions. It was composed presumably in 1795, shortly after the first draft of Herbst's catalogue was finished.

MANUSCRIPTS. LITITZ. Holograph parts — C pr., C sec., A, B, Vlo I/II, Vla, Vlc., Org.

No. 90.2.
ER WIRD DIR GNÄDIG SEYN, WENN DU RUFEST P.

Langsam 3/4, 63 meas. 4 interl. of 3 meas. each, postl. 3 meas. e min.

Pretty poor anthem. The fact that I N copied the piece makes it clear that there was a holograph older than the present one.

MANUSCRIPTS.

LITITZ. Holograph parts — C pr. I/II, C sec. I/II, A I/II, B I/II, Vlo I/II, Vla, Vlc.

BETHLEHEM. I N — see *Der in euch angefangen hat* (No. 68.3); H W — C pr., C sec., A, B, Vlo I/II, Vla, B, Org.; C F S — C pr.; add. — C sec.

No. 91.1.
DAST IST EIN KÖSTLICH DING, DEM HERRN DANKEN P.

Vivace 2/4, 88 meas. Prel. 16, interl. 3 and 5, postl. 13 meas. A maj.

Lively anthem of not extraordinary quality. Three of the four anthems included in No. 91 were copied by H W with the indication *Zum 4ten May 1796*. All four presumably were written in that year.

MANUSCRIPTS.

LITITZ. Holograph parts of 1.-4. — C pr., C sec., A, B, Vlo I/II, Vla, Vlc., Org. 4 vocal parts: Coro II, for 1. and 4. only; add. — C pr. for 1. only.

BETHLEHEM. H W — Two sets of parts, one dated *Zum 4ten May 1796*, both including C pr., C sec., A, B, Vlo I/II, Vla, Org.; C F S — C pr., C sec., A, B; add. parts by TILL and later.

No. 91.2.
ICH LASSE DICH NICHT, DU SEGNEST MICH DENN P.

Larghetto 6/8, 58 meas. Interl. 5 and several short ones, postl. 5. A maj.

In perfect correspondence to the text which continues with a poem after the Bible quotation, the music starts with the chorus, and adds an interlude after the first sentence. This is a regular anthem, not uninteresting.

MANUSCRIPTS.

BETHLEHEM. H W — two sets of parts, one dated *Zum 4ten May 1796,* both including C pr., C sec., A, B, Vlo I/II, Vla, B, Org.; 2 add. — C pr. by TILL.

NAZARETH. Vlo II, Vla, Vlc., B, Org. only.

No. 91.3.
DENNOCH WERDEN WIR BEYM GLÄUBEN P.

Andantino 2/4, 53 meas. Interl. 5, postl. 3 meas. D maj.
Modest anthem.

MANUSCRIPTS. No parts in addition to those mentioned in No. 91.1.

No. 91.4.
DER GOTT DES FRIEDENS HEILIGE EUCH DURCH UND DURCH P.

Moderato 2/2, 76 meas. Prel. 10, interl. twice 5, postl. 6 meas. C maj.

Energetic regular anthem.

MANUSCRIPTS.

LITITZ. H W — C pr., C sec., A, B, Vlo I/II, Vla, B, Org. The call number of the manuscript indicates that it actually belongs to the material from Bethlehem. Add. — C pr., C sec. 2 later C pr.

BETHLEHEM. H W — C pr., C sec., A, B, Vlo I/II, Vla, B, Org. *Zum 4ten May 1796.* C pr., C sec., A, B, the beginning changed to *Nun der Gott p.* Add parts by C F S and TILL.

In GRACEHAM catalogue.

No. 101.2.
ICH WOHNE UNTER MEINEM VOLK P.

Angenehm 2/4, 37 meas., including prel. of 8, short inter., and postl. of 5 meas. Bedächtig 3/4, 34 meas., including postl. of 3 meas. F maj.

Regular anthem, without exceptional quality.

MANUSCRIPTS.

LITITZ. Holograph parts — C pr., C sec., A, B, Vlo I/II, Vla, Vlc., Org.; add. parts — C pr., C sec., C pr., B later.

BETHLEHEM. H W — C pr., C sec., A, B, Vlo I/II, Vla (B and Org. missing).

Score in LANCASTER catalogue.

No. 101.3.
ALSO SPRICHT DER HOHE UND ERHABENE P.

Langsam C, 41 meas., including prel. of 6 and postl. of 5 meas.
Mässig munter 3/4, 22 meas., including postl. of 3 meas. c min.

The first part, with a well written prelude and postlude, is kept
mostly in halfnotes and quarternotes. The setting is dignified and
effective. The second part offers less of interest.

MANUSCRIPTS. Holograph parts as above; add. parts include C pr., C pr. II, C sec. II, A II. Single part in Bethlehem
see No. 101.4.

In LANCASTER catalogue.

No. 101.4.
SELIG SIND, DIE REINES HERZENS SIND P.

Moderato 2/2, 89 meas. Interl. of 2, 3, 3, postl. of 3 meas.
B fl. maj.

This piece is similar in style to a liturgy. The Chorus starts at
the very beginning, the instrumental parts not being independent.
After 44 measures the Chorale *Wie schön leucht' uns der Mor-
genstern,* in the original version (not in the one Gregor chooses)
is used for three lines. This unique quotation is preceded and
divided by an interl. of 3 meas. and followed by one of 4. The
last section of the piece starts with a free recapitulation.

MANUSCRIPTS. Holograph parts as in No. 101.1. Add. — 2
C pr. and later parts.

BETHLEHEM. H W — 1.) out of a series of three pieces,
the others being lost, C pr., C sec., A, B, Vlo I. 2.) independent
set, C pr., C sec., A, B, Vlo I/II, Vla, B, Org. Add. parts by
C F S and later.

No. 102.1.
HEILIG, SELIG IST DIE FREUNDSCHAFT UND
GEMEINSCHAFT P.

Affettuoso 2/4, 94 meas. After 44 meas. etwas munterer. Prel.
8, interl. 5 and 9, postl. 8 meas. E fl. maj.

One of Herbst's best compositions written in Europe (see I.
No. 90) and presented here in a second version. The prelude is
well knit, the setting carefully done, the instruments being rather
independent and attractively used.

MANUSCRIPTS.

LITITZ. Holograph parts — Vlo I/II, Vla, Vlc., Org.

BETHLEHEM. PETER — C pr. I/II, C sec. I/II, A I/II.
B I/II, Vlo I/II, Vla, Vlc., Org. Several add. parts.

No. 104.1.
ICH GEHE EINHER IN DER KRAFT DES HERRN P.

Andante 3/4, 56 meas. Prel. 13, interl. 3 and 5, postl. 3 meas. F maj.

A solo for Soprano with strings and organ, with fine and original details, very carefully worked out. The accompaniment stands out among Herbst's best pieces. The composition is included in the first number of the series of Music of the American Moravians.

MANUSCRIPTS.

LITITZ. Holograph parts — C pr., Vlo I/II, Vla, Vlc., Org.

BETHLEHEM. PETER — 2 C pr. solo (!), Vlo I/II, Vla, Vlc., Org. Copied presumably 1808.

No. 105.1.
ICH FREUE MICH IN DEM HERRN, UND MEINE SEELE IST FRÖHLICH P.

Vivace 3/8, 85 meas. Prel. 10, interl. 5, Soprano solo 4, interl. 6, postl. 6 meas. B fl. maj.

The composition recalls the contemporary minuet type.

MANUSCRIPTS. LITITZ. Holograph parts — C pr., C sec. incompl., B, Vlo I/II, Vla, Vlc., Org. The other parts are missing. Add. parts — 6 C pr., C sec., B, later.

No. 107.2.
SO SPRICHT DER HERR: SIEHE ICH VERTILGE DEINE MISSETHAT WIE EINE WOLKE P.

Lebhaft, doch nicht zu geschwind C, 31 meas. Prel. 4, interl. 2, postl. 2 meas. F maj.

Regular anthem of average quality. Possibly copied from a European original.

MANUSCRIPTS.

LITITZ. G G M — C pr., C sec., A, B, Vlo I/II, Vla, Vlc., Org. Add. — C pr., C sec., A, B.

BETHLEHEM. V VL — C pr., C sec., A, B, Vlo I/II, Vla, Vlc., Org. Several add. parts.

NAZARETH. H W — C pr., C sec., A, B, Vlo I/II, Vla, Vlc., Org. Add. parts later.

In GRACEHAM catalogue.

No. 108.

1.) BLESSED SHALT THOU BE, WHEN THOU COMEST IN P.

Moderato 2/4, 49 meas. Prel. 8, duo Canti 19, interl. 4, postl. 4 meas. G maj.

2.) PRAISE THE LORD, O JERUSALEM, PRAISE THY LORD, O ZION P.

Vivace 2/4, 84 meas. Prel. 9, interl. 2 and 3, postl. 3 meas. At several places the C pr. or the two Canti alone.

The pieces, which are the only anthems with English words extant in the Northern province, exemplify well Herbst's style in this period. They were written presumably around 1800. Especially the second is lively and attractive.

MANUSCRIPT. LITITZ. Holograph parts — C pr., C sec., A, B, Vlo I/II, Vla, Vlc., Org. The vocal parts are marked Coro II, in a handwriting different from Herbst's. The parts of the first chorus are lost.

No. 111.1.

WIR SIND GLIEDER SEINES LEIBES P.

Mässig 2/4, 52 meas. Prel. 8, interl. 4, postl. 3 meas. F maj. Regular anthem of modest quality.

MANUSCRIPTS.

LITITZ. Holograph parts (to 1.-3.) — C pr., C sec., A, B, Vlo I/II, Vla, Vlc., Org.; add. (to 1. and 2.) — C pr.

BETHLEHEM. V VL — C pr., C sec., A, B, Vlo I/II, Vla, Vlc., Org. C F S — 2 C pr., 2 C sec., 2 A, B.

No. 111.2.

AUF SEIN VOLLGÜLTIGS BLUTVERGIESSEN P.

Etwas lebhaft 2/4, 59 meas. Prel. 9, interl. 7, postl. 7 meas. A maj.

Throughout in the more modern style Herbst cultivated in his later years.

MANUSCRIPTS.

LITITZ. Holograph parts — see No. 111.1. Unidentified writer — Coro II: C pr., C sec., A, B, Add. — Org.

BETHLEHEM. V VL — C pr., C sec., A, B, Vlo I/II, Vla, Vlc., Org. C F S — C pr., C sec., A, B. Several add. parts.

No. 111.3.
SCHÄTZT RECHT HOCH DAS ANGENEHME P.

Angenehm 3/8, 68 meas. Prel. 8, interl. twice 4, postl. 4 meas.
G maj.

Herbst indicates on his title-page that a second text *O benutzt
die angenehme segensreiche Gnadenzeit* could also be used with
the present piece. He added the second text to his vocal parts
himself.

MANUSCRIPTS.

LITITZ. Holograph parts — see No. 111.1. Add. — 2 C pr..
C sec., A.

BETHLEHEM. Parts by V VL and C F S as to No. 111.2.
Add. — C pr.

NAZARETH. H W — C pr., C sec., A, B, Vlo I/II, Vla, Vlc.
A second set of vocal parts.

No. 112.
GNADE, FRIED UND SELIGKEIT KOMM AUS JESU TOD UND SCHMERZEN P.

Etwas langsam 3/4, 39 meas. Postl. 3 meas. D maj.

Scarcely interesting composition. In Herbst's vocal parts, a
second beginning *Gnad und Segen, Trost und Freud* is added.

MANUSCRIPTS.

LITITZ. Holograph parts — C pr. I/II, C sec. I/II, A I/II,
B I/II, Vlo I/II, Vla, Vlc., Org.; add. — 2 C pr.

BETHLEHEM. H W — 2 C pr., 2 C sec., T, 2 B, Vlo I/II,
Vla, B, Org.; add. parts — by TILL and later.

No. 119.1.
GOTT HAT UNTER UNS AUFGERICHTET DAS WORT VON DER VERSÖHNUNG.

Davon soll in der Gemein, die Er durch Sein Blut erworben—
Tag und Nacht kein Schweigen seyn.
Gott ward Mensch, und ist gestorben,
Volk des Herrn, für dich! Dess freue dich ewiglich.

Text Verse Br. Ges. B. 1.3.

Mässig lebhaft C, 113 meas. Prel. 13, interl. 10, postl. 2.
Several soli for the first soprano. D maj.

This composition has a special historic interest as it was used
for the inauguration of the church at Bethlehem, May 20, 1806.
Both organ copies at Bethlehem mention this fact. The program
of the service which is handed down in several copies confirms
the statement.

Herbst's holograph does not mention the fact that the music was used for the inauguration of the church at Bethlehem. It is, however, probable that Herbst composed the piece especially for the festival for which it was used. The inauguration was celebrated with several services, in German as well as in English. During the evening service Herbst himself took the part of minister and preacher.

The music of the organ reduction which is reproduced in the appendix, plates P to S, shows Herbst's later, more fluent and florid style. The piece is carefully contrived, melodious, and harmonically as well as formally well built. It proves, on the other hand, good craftsmanship rather than ingenuity, and scarcely deserves a place among Herbst's best creations.

MANUSCRIPTS.

LITITZ. Holograph parts — C pr., C sec., A, B, B II, Fl. I/II, Co. I/II in D, Vlo I/II, Vla, Vlc., Org.; add. — C pr.

BETHLEHEM. PETER and C F S jointly, the former writing the instrumental parts, the latter the vocal parts and the title which indicates *zur Einweyhung des neuen Kirchensaals in Bethlehem 1806* — 2 C pr., C sec., CA, CB, Fl. I/II, Co. I/II in D, Vlo I/II, Vla, Vlc., Org.; C F S (a second set of parts, possibly intended for a congregation abroad) — 2 C pr., 2 C sec., CA, CB, Vlo I/II, Vla, Vlc., Org. It gives the exact date *Bethlehem d. 20ten May 1806.* Possibly the set was supplemented about 1813 when a second piece was added.

NAZARETH. H W — C pr., C sec., A, B, Fl. I/II, Co. I/II in D, Vlo I/II, Vla, Vlc., Org. Later add. parts.

No. 122.1.
KOMMT LASSET UNS ZUM HERREN FÜGEN P.

This composition is not by Herbst as the title-page makes evident. A Bethlehem copy erroneously indicates Herbst as composer.

No. 125.2.
DIS IST EIN TAG, DEN DER HERR GEMACHT HAT P.

Fröhlich 3/8, 81 meas. Prel. 12, interl. 10, postl. 10 meas. G maj.

Solo for Soprano with strings and organ. Among the few examples of its type among Herbst's compositions, it holds it own well.

The paper Herbst used for this and a few other manuscripts of this period, is larger than usual and looks similar to that of his European manuscripts. It is, however, even larger, and has no watermark. Although the paper looks much older we must assume that it does not go further back than the beginning of the 19th century.

MANUSCRIPT. LITITZ. Holograph parts — C pr. and Org. independent, Vlo I/II, Vla and Vlc. on the back of parts to *Es ist vollbracht* by Haydn, written by Peter.

No. 126.1.
DAS BLUT JESU CHRISTI, DES SOHNES GOTTES, MACHT UNS REIN VON ALLER SÜNDE.

Andante C, 64 meas. Prel. 10, interl. 4, postl. 5 meas. F maj. Melodious, soft composition, well contrived.

MANUSCRIPT. LITITZ. Holograph parts — 2 C pr., 2 C sec., 2 A, 2 B, Vlo I/II, Vla, Vlc., Org. Unusually large 8vo, as in 125.2.

No. 140.1.
WIE LIEBLICH, TRÖSTEND UND WIE MILD WIRD HIER DAS BLÖDE HERZIERFÜLLT P.

Affettuoso, Adagio C, 64 meas. Prel. 8, interl. 2 and 3, postl. 3. c min.

This fine composition is in the style of a choral aria rather than an anthem. It has similarity with *Solange wir hienieden wallen* and shows the same quality. It introduces a recapitulation of 8 meas., with a nice codetta, reminding of the recitative *Hier schläft es.*

MANUSCRIPTS.

LITITZ. Holograph parts — C pr. I/II, C sec. I/II, A I/II, B I/II, Vlo I/II, Vla, Vlc., Org.

BETHLEHEM. C F S — 3 C pr., 3 C sec., 2 A, B, Vlo I/II, Vla, Vlc., with Org. by PETER; add. — A, and later parts.

No. 141.1.
DU BIST KOMMEN ZU DEM BERGE ZION P.

Mässig lebhaft C, 75 meas. Interl. three times 4, postl. 4 meas. F maj.

Good regular anthem. It was copied for Bethlehem in 1808 and apparently composed in that year, being the last dated composition of Herbst's, except the second version of *Freuet euch und seid fröhlich* which presumably was written in 1810. Its style is more delicate than brilliant, the setting fine and attractive.

MANUSCRIPTS.

LITITZ. Holograph parts — C pr. I/II, C sec. I/II, A I/II,
B I/II, Vlo I/II, Vla, Vlc., Org.

BETHLEHEM. C F S — 4 C pr., 2 C sec., 2 A, 2 B, Vlo I/II,
Vla, Vlc., Org.

No. 141.2.
DA WERDET IHR SINGEN WIE AN EINEM HEILIGEN ABEND P.

Vivace, nicht zu geschwind, 2/2, 66 meas. Prel. 8, interl. and
postl. 5 meas. C maj.

Good anthem of advanced style, similar to the preceding, and
evidently written at the same time.

MANUSCRIPTS.

LITITZ. Holograph parts — as in No. 141.1.

BETHLEHEM. H W — 2 C pr., 2 C sec., 2 A, 2 B, Vlo I/II.
Vla, B, Org.

No. 143.1.
SO LANGE WIR HIENIEDEN WALLEN, SEY UNSRE SORGE TAG UND NACHT P.

Andante C, 74 meas. Prel. 4, interl. 4 and 4, postl. 4 meas.
F maj.

One of Herbst's most delicate pieces, especially fine in its
melodic lines. It is remarkably similar to the more intimate
compositions of Peter. The excellent bass leading should be
mentioned.

MANUSCRIPTS.

LITITZ. Holograph parts — C pr. I/II. C sec. I/II, A I/II,
B I/II, Vlo I/II, Vla, Vlc., Org.; add. — C pr.

BETHLEHEM. C F S — 4 C pr., 3 C sec., 2 A, B, Vlo I/II,
Vla, Vlc.; Org. by PETER.

No. 143.2.
HIER BLEIBEN JESU HEILGE WUNDEN P.

Larghetto 3/4, 63 meas. Prel. 8, interl. 8, postl. 5 meas. A maj.
Simple, melodious anthem without exceptional details.

MANUSCRIPTS.

LITITZ. Holograph parts as in No. 143.1. Later add. parts.

BETHLEHEM. PETER — 2 C pr., 2 C sec., 2 A, 2 B, Vlo
I/II, Vla, Vlc., Org.; add. — parts by C F S and later.

No. 143.3.
AMEN, RUHM, DANK, PREIS UND EHRE P.

Allegro maestoso C, 85 meas. Prel. 19, interl. twice 4, postl. 2 meas. D maj.

Major anthem, with abundant use of dotted eighth notes and sixteenths. A second text to this composition is *Lob sey Christo in der Höhe.*

MANUSCRIPTS.

LITITZ. Holograph parts — as in No. 143.1., Fl. I/II and Co. I/II in D; add. — C pr. and later add. parts.

BETHLEHEM. C F S — 4 S, 2 A, T, B, Fl. I/II, Co. I/II in D. Vlo I/II, Vla, Vlc., Org. by TILL; several add. parts.

No. 144.1.
KINDLEIN! BLEIBET BEY IHM P.

Mässig C, 105 meas. Prel. 10, interl. 6, 3 meas. B fl. maj.

A melodious and carefully written composition. The last section starts with a shortened recapitulation of 16 measures, after which a free continuation is given.

MANUSCRIPTS.

LITITZ. Holograph parts — C pr. I/II, C sec. I/II, A II, T, B I/II, Vlo I/II, Vla, Vlc., Org.

BETHLEHEM. PETER — C pr. I/II, C sec. I/II, A I/II, B I/II, Vlo I/II, Vla, Vlc., Org.; add. — parts by C F S, and a single C sec. II.

No. 146.1.
DAS VOLK, DAS IM FINSTERN WANDELT, SIEHET EIN GROSSES LICHT P.

Larghetto andante C, 84 meas. Prel. 4, B solo 11 and 7, interl. 5 and 3, postl. 6. After 28 meas. Etwas geschwinder. d min.

This composition which appears as No. 10 of the Music of the American Moravians may be considered as Herbst's most striking composition. It is rich in its melodic material, harmonically interesting, and makes excellent use of syncopations in the accompaniment.

C. F. Schaaff who wrote the title page to an organ part by Peter indicates that this composition was *di Johs. Herbst verbessert.* No first version of it was found, however, and it is quite probable that Schaaff mistook an indication which referred to the following composition only, as being meant for the present one too. Most probably, this is one of Herbst's last independent works.

MANUSCRIPTS.

LITITZ. Holograph parts — S, C pr. II, C sec. II, A I/II, T I, B I/II, the parts of the first chorus without indication Coro I; Vlo I/II, Vla, Vlc., Org.

BETHLEHEM. C F S — 4 C pr., 2 A, T, B, Vlo I/II, Vla, Vlc., Org. by PETER. All parts, the Org. excepted, on the back of the following piece, the title-page covering both.

No. 146.2.
LOBET DEN HERRN, ALLE HEIDEN P.

Munter, nur nicht zu geschwind C, 26 meas., 30 and 18 meas. C maj.

This is the first of a series of second versions which Herbst made of earlier compositions shortly before he left Lititz. The first version of this composition is not handed down in a manuscript by Herbst himself, but in a set of parts written by Nitschmann who died in 1791. Presumably this version was written in Europe. The second version is handed down in holograph parts as well as in a Bethlehem copy by Schaaff and Peter, the title-page to which indicates *di Johs. Herbst verbessert*. Probably this was written at about the same time as the copy of the second version of Herbst's *Freuet euch und seyd fröhlich*, which is dated 1810.

The two versions do not differ greatly as far as the formal and harmonic structure is concerned. A free da capo form is used. In the second version, the middle section is augmented by two measures, due to improvements of the melodic and harmonic setting. Most important changes, however, occur in the accompaniment. The first violin part of both versions is reproduced in the appendix, plates T and U. One will notice that, while the earlier version is quite modest and old-fashioned, the later one is quite similar in style to the brilliant instrumental parts which Peter applied to his sacred compositions, ever since he started to compose. Herbst has copied only a few of Peter's compositions, and he was scarcely influenced by the considerably younger musician, but he had to yield to the development of musical style in general. It might be, however, that the example of G. G. Müller who lived, for many years, close to Herbst, partly accounts for the astonishing changes Herbst's style underwent in the last years of his life.

MANUSCRIPTS.

First version. Bethlehem only. I N — C pr., C sec., A, CB, Vlo I/II, Vla, B; V VL — C pr., C sec., A, B, Vlo I/II, Vla, Vlc.; H W — Org.

Second version. LITITZ. Holograph parts — as in No. 146.1. Ob.o Fl.(!) I/II, and Co. I/II in C.

BETHLEHEM. C F S — as in No. 146.1. Ob.o Fl. I/II, Co. I/II in C.; Org. by PETER.

No. 147.1.
DER HERR IST UNSER KÖNIG P.

Allegro moderato C, 124 meas. Prel. 17, interl. twice 6, post. 2 meas. D maj.

Another second version, made by Herbst in his last years. The first version was included in the music *Zum 13ten November 1767* —see I, No. 96. Neither there nor in his catalogue does Herbst reveal himself as the composer, and as the title page of the second version is lost, we may not be absolutely sure whether Peter's attribution can be trusted. Peter, on the other hand, must have seen the complete original manuscript, and as Herbst made fundamental changes in the composition when he wrote the second version, the conclusion that he was the author of the first one also seems quite safe.

Among Herbst's compositions, the present one is exceptional. The first theme has a really majestic character. The prelude, with an excellent bass, and the first part of the choral section are outstanding. The first part is recapitulated within the last third, the form being well rounded out. In contrast to the first version, Herbst has doubled the value of the notes, giving the composition a quicker and more freely running motion, to which minor changes are added. As in the previous composition, a group of wind instruments makes the second version more colorful.

MANUSCRIPTS.

LITITZ. Holograph parts — Org. only, without title page, and incomplete.

BETHLEHEM. PETER — C pr., C pr. I and C pr. II, C sec. and C sec. II, A II, T(I), B I, Fl. I/II, Co. I/II in D, Vlo I/II, Vla, Vlc., Org.; C pr. and C pr. II by TILL; later add. A.

NAZARETH. C pr., C sec., A, T, B, Fl. I/II, Vlo I/II, Vla, Vlc.

No. 148.1
HALLELUJAH LASST UNS SINGEN P.

Moderato C, 126 meas. Prel. 23, interl. 8, postl. 9 meas. E fl. maj.

This extended composition which might be Herbst's latest creation, is unusual in several respects. At several places it uses a solo trio of 2 clarinets and a bassoon. The chorus starts in unison, without instruments. The style is more monumental than in almost any of Herbst's anthems. It might be that Herbst was

influenced here by compositions by Bechler. Herbst himself
copied several of these in his later years, and a note in Bechler's
hand appears on the first page of the organ part. Bechler himself
copied the present composition.

MANUSCRIPTS.

LITITZ. Holograph parts — S, C pr. II, C sec. II, A I/II, T,
B I/II, Clar. I/II in B fl., Fag., Co. I/II in E fl., Vlo I/II, Vla,
Vlc., Org. Several add. parts, including a Fl.

BETHLEHEM. WOLLE, late copy — 4 S, 4 A, 2 T, 2 B,
2 Clar., Fag., Co. I/II, Vlo I/II, Vla, Vlc., and Fondamento.
Later add. Fl.

NAZARETH. BECHLER — A, B, Clar. I/II, Fag., Co. I/II,
Vlo I/II, Vla, Vlc., Org. Later vocal parts.

No. 148.2.

FREUET UND SEYD FRÖHLICH, DIE IHR SEINEN TAG SEHET P.

Lebhaft, doch nicht zu geschwind 3/4, 124 meas. Prel. 14,
interl. 5, 4, 6, 4, postl. 7 meas. C maj.

Herbst has made two settings of the present text. The first
one is handed down in his *Music zum 24ten December 1767* (see
I, No. 97). The second one belongs to his latest works. Herbst
mentions it in the catalogue as *verbessert*. C. F. Schaaff, who
made a copy for Bethlehem, wrote correspondingly on the cover
Di Johs Herbst vermehrt u. verbessert 1810.. The second version
of the present composition is in its first parts almost entirely
independent from the first one, but follows it closely in the last
section. It requires clarinets, and a bassoon, as the preceding
anthem, in addition to the two horns which appear more often
in Herbst's composition. The anthem is energetic and a worthy
piece.

MANUSCRIPTS.

LITITZ. Holograph parts — as in No. 148.1. No add. parts
except a later Org.

BETHLEHEM. C F S — 5 C pr., 2 C sec., 3 A, T, B, Clar. in
B fl., 2 Co. in C, Vlo I/II, Vla, Vlc.; Org. by PETER. Later
add. parts.

No. 149.2.

DER IN EUCH ANGEFANGEN HAT DAS GUTE WERK P.

Lebhaft, 2/4, 56 meas. Prel. 11, interl. 5, postl. 2 meas. C maj.

A quite modest composition, possibly not as late as the catalogue number would seem to indicate.

MANUSCRIPTS.

LITITZ. Holograph parts — C pr. I/II, C sec. I/II, A I/II, B I/II, Vlo I/II, Vla, Vlc., Org., the parts of Coro II possibly added afterwards. Add. — C pr. and a later Fl.

BETHLEHEM. H W — C pr., C sec., A, B, Vlo I/II, Vla, B, Org.; add. — 3 C pr., 2 C sec. by TILL.

III.

COMPOSITIONS IN THE BETHLEHEM COLLECTION ATTRIBUTED TO HERBST

(No holographs preserved, no copies in Lititz collection)

1.
AUF, SEELE, SCHICKE DICH P.

An Arietta to which Peter wrote variations. See under his name, No. 528, and the appendix, plate 00.

2. No. 511.2.
DER HERR HAT ZION ERWÄHLET P.

Moderato 3/4, 56 meas. Interl. 8 meas. C maj.

MANUSCRIPT. H W — C pr., C sec., T, B, Vlo I/II, Vla, B; Org. by PETER; C F S — 2 C pr., 2 C sec., T.

3. No. 509.
DER HERR ZABAOTH WIRD KÖNIG SEYN P.

Munter 2/2, 31 meas. No instrumental sections. D maj.

MANUSCRIPTS. H W — 3 C pr., 2 C sec., T, B, Vlo I/II, Vla, B.

4. No. 489.
DIE GNADE UND WAHRHEIT DES HERRN P.

Allegro moderato 2/2, 62 meas. B fl. maj.

MANUSCRIPT. PETER — 2 C pr. I/II, C sec. I/II, A I/II, B I, Vlo I/II, Vla, Vlc., Org.; add. — C sec. and B.

5. No. 82.4.
FREUE DICH DEINER HÜTTEN P.

Lebhaft 3/8, 46 meas.; 2/4, 35 meas. Prel. 20, S solo 10, postl. to first section 10 meas. Interl. in second section 4 and 7, postl. 5 meas. D maj.

The structure would seem quite unusual within Herbst's compositions. The present piece appears, however, in the earliest Bethlehem catalogue.

MANUSCRIPT. I N — C pr., C sec., A, CB, Vlo I/II, Vla, B.

6. No. 503(?)
FREUET EUCH GOTTES, EURES HEILANDES P.

Allegretto C, 64 meas. Prel. 18, solo 4, duo 8, interl. 2, postl. 3 meas. D maj.

The aspect of the florid music as well as of Peter's material leads to the conclusion that this might be one of Herbst's later compositions.

MANUSCRIPT. PETER — 2 C pr. I, 2 C pr. II, 2 C sec. II, A I/II, B, Vlo I/II, Vla, Vlc., Org.

7. No. 247.
GOTT KOMMT UND WIRD EUCH HELFEN P.

Andante 2/4, 47 meas. Prel. 10, interl. 3, postl. 3 meas. A maj. In earliest Bethlehem catalogue.

MANUSCRIPT. H W — C pr., C sec., A, B, Vlo I/II, Vla, B, Org.; later add. parts.

8. No. 240.
GOTT, MAN LOBET DICH IN DER STILLE P.

Mässig geschwind 2/2, 20 meas. C maj.; 25 meas. F maj.; 36 meas. C maj.

Free da capo form without interludes. Included in earliest Bethlehem catalogue.

MANUSCRIPT. H W — C pr., C sec, A, B, Ob. I/II, Fag., Vlo I/II, Vla, Vlc., Org.; add. parts by TILL.

9. No. 228.
HEILIGET GOTT DEN HERRN IN EUREN HERZEN P.

Larghetto 2/2, 47 meas. Prel. 5, interl. 5, postl. 5 meas. E fl. maj.

An excellent composition, melodically striking, well harmonized and balanced, with an impressively steady pace. The attribution to Herbst is presumably right. The composition may belong in the neighborhood of *Er hat in den Tagen seines Fleisches* (see after I. No. 97) or of *Fürwahr, Er trug unsere Krankheit* (see I. No. 172). Mentioned in the earliest catalogue.

MANUSCRIPT. I N — C pr., C sec., A, CB, Vlo I/II, Vla, B. Org. by H W.

10. No. 345.

IHR SEYD DAS AUSERWÄHLTE GESCHLECHT P.

Moderato 2/2, 58 meas. Interl. 5 and 3, postl. 2 meas. B fl. maj.

MANUSCRIPT. I N — third piece in a set of vocal parts only, following Danket dem HErrn. In old Bethlehem catalogue, Lititz catalogue red series 189.2, Salem catalogue.

11. No. 354.

NACHDEM DIE KINDER FLEISCH UND BLUT HABEN P.

Bedächtig 3/4, 99 meas. Prel. 11, interl. 6, postl. 10 meas. D maj.

Attribution to Herbst in earliest Bethlehem catalogue, but possibly by mistake. In the original set, written by Nitschmann, the preceding composition and the following were by Herbst.

MANUSCRIPT. Only Org. by TILL, together with *Gott war in Christo*, and 2 C pr., B by C F S preserved.

12. No. 493.

O HERR, DU ERFORSCHEST UND KENNEST UNS P.

2/2. Recitat(ivo) Accom(agnato), 10 meas.; Tactmässig, 10 meas.; Etwas geschwinder, 15 meas.; Langsamer, 3 meas.; Munterer, 15 meas. B fl. maj.

This strange composition is certainly not written by Herbst. It starts with a declaiming section, a Recitativo for the entire chorus, somewhat in the style of a liturgy, which also influenced the author in writing the following sections. The quicker sections close with a pedalpoint of the dominant above which a continuous sequence of suspensions goes down from the 7th and 9th through an octave and a half. At the beginning of Munterer a similar sequence with suspensions on the weak beat are given. The entire piece evidently was composed by someone who had little knowledge of theory, but no lack of imagination. Here we may see before us a remnant of the earliest music written at Bethlehem. There is, however, no proof for this conjecture.

MANUSCRIPT. H W — C pr., 2 C sec., 2 A, B, Vlo I/II, Vla, B, Org. Judging from the appearance of paper and handwriting this must be one of Hanna Weber's first attempts at music copying which may go back to about 1790.

13. No. 357.
SELIG SIND DIE TODTEN, DIE IN DEM HERRN STERBEN P.

Andante 2/2, 76 meas. Prel. 12, interl. 4, postl. 6 meas. G maj.

An expressive and dignified composition. The strings, Semper piano con sordino, have a fine independent accompaniment in eighth notes. In earliest Bethlehem, and in Salem catalogues.

MANUSCRIPTS. I N — 1., together with *Ehre sey unserm Heiland* (see I No. 330) and *Singet dem Herrn* (No. 48.2) A, Vlo I/II, Vla, B; 2. independently, C pr., C sec., A, CB, Vlo I/II, Vla, B.; Org. by V VL; C F S — 2 C pr., C sec., A. CB.

14. No. 303 (?)
SIE WERDEN WEDER HUNGERN NOCH DÜRSTEN P.

A single sheet in fol. includes on one page the above title which, according to the earliest and newer catalogues of the Bethlehem collection is by Herbst. The indication Affectuoso is given, but no music left. H W's handwriting, a sheet belonging to fol. 56.

12. No. 420.
SIEHE, DER BRÄUTIGAM KOMMT, GEHET AUS. IHM ENTGEGEN P.

Lebhaft 3/4, 46 meas. F maj.; Etwas munterer, 7 meas. Recitativisch 2/2, 24 meas.; Munter 3/4, 13 meas. B fl. maj.

In the style of a liturgy. Attribution to Herbst presumably erroneous.

MANUSCRIPT. H W — 3 C pr.. 2 C sec., 2 A, B, Vlo I/II, Vla, B, Org.; add. — C pr. and C sec. by C F S.

13. No. 369.
SINGET, IHR ERLÖSTEN, SINGT GROSS UND KLEIN P.

Lebhaft 3/4, 90 meas. Prel. 8, interl. 9, postl. 3 meas. D maj.

A vivacious composition of good harmonic structure, and with a fine interlude. The Bethlehem manuscript presents the piece in an arrangement for two antiphonal choruses; there are, however, no sections with more than 4 actual parts. The attribution to Herbst is probably right. The composition may belong in the same period as *Gehe hin mit Frieden* (see II No. 78.2) with which it appears in the manuscript.

MANUSCRIPT. V VL — C pr. I/II, C sec. I/II, A I/II, B I/II, Vlo I/II, Vla, Vlc., Org. The differentiation of Coro I and Coro II is given by underlining, the music text being identical for the corresponding voices. Add. — C pr. II by H W and another by C F S.

14. No. 538.
SO OFT WIR IN ERWARTUNG STEHEN P.

Etwas langsam 2/4, 63 meas. Prel. 5, interl. 3, 3 and 4, postl. 2 meas. F maj.

A fine example of Herbst's more intimate compositions. The melody as well as the harmonic setting are carefully chosen, and touching. Specially good instrumental endings.

MANUSCRIPT. PETER and C F S — together with *Auf, Seele, schicke dich* which is discussed as a composition by Peter. Add. — Vlc.

15. No. 489.
WEIL IHR DENN KINDER SEYD P.

Larghetto 3/4, 50 meas. Etwas langsamer, 13 meas. F maj.

Copied together with *Die Gnade und Wahrheit des Herrn*. In earliest Bethlehem, and Salem catalogues. Not outstanding, probably European composition by Herbst.

MANUSCRIPT. PETER — 2 C pr. I/II, C sec. I/II, A I/II, B I, Vlo I/II, Vla, Vlc., Org.

16. No. 235.
WIR SEGNEN EUCH, DIE IHR VOM HAUSE DES HERRN SEYD P.

Andante 2/2, 44 meas. Prel. 8, interl. 4, postl. 5 meas. F maj.

A simple composition without interesting details. In earliest Bethlehem, and Salem catalogue. Presumably European composition by Herbst.

MANUSCRIPT. I N — C pr., C sec (in A clef), A (in T clef), CB, Vlo I/II, Vla, B.; Org. by H W; Add. — 3 C pr., C sec. II by C F S.

DAVID MORITZ MICHAEL

David Moritz Michael was born at Kienhausen near Erfurt, October 27, 1751. He came to America in 1795. He was first stationed at Nazareth, and later on at Bethlehem. "When the Brethren's House was given up in 1814," Grider remarks in a note on a portrait of Michael, "he again returned to Europe where he died." Michael's death occurred at Neuwied in 1825.

As a performer, Michael must have been the most efficient of all the musicians who played an important role in the musical life of the Moravian settlements. He is remembered as a good violinist, and as a man who could play almost any wind instrument. He is said to have played duets on French horns. The collection of the Moravian Historical Society at Nazareth preserves a *Verzeichniss derer Musicalien welche im Concert sind gemacht worden* which runs consecutively from October 14, 1796 until 1825, and includes a few later entries. Apparently it was Michael whose activity started this series of concerts. He is also mentioned as the leader of the memorable performance of Haydn's "Creation" in 1811, for which Peter copied out the parts.

Michael was specially interested in music for wind instruments. The collections from Lititz and Bethlehem include 13 *Partien* for wind instruments, for 2 clarinets, 1 or 2 bassoons, 2 horns, and an occasional flute or trumpet. Whether these suites were composed in Europe, or in America, we cannot say. But there are two more compositions for wind instruments which were evidently composed for Bethlehem. Grider gives a colorful account of the boat ride for which one of the compositions was expressly written. Grider explains that the music followed a certain programme. While the original music for the *Wasserfahrt auf der Lecha* does not conform with Grider's description, a suite of three *Partien* handed down in Bethlehem only apparently was the composition Grider's story refers to. It would seem that the original music for the boat ride which required 2 bassoons, was not programmatic, and that Michael composed a second, programmatic set of pieces for a similar occasion, when he could count on one bassoon player only.

All of Michael's compositions are quite poor. They display an extreme lack of imagination. Modulations are rare, the melodic lines commonplace nearly throughout, the metrical structure always most simple. This is true for Michael's sacred as well as secular compositions none of which would be worth while reviving. The vocal compositions are clearly divided into larger pieces which are described here as Anthems, and short, modest hymns, which are collected here as Ariettas, which term was used occasionally by the later American Moravian composers. Michael's handwriting rarely appears in the copies of his compositions which were mostly made by C F S, H W and TILL; apparently Michael kept the originals, which were not very clearly written, himself. The handwriting of evident holographs only is mentioned in the following list. Manuscripts without further indication belong to the original Bethlehem collection.

Anthems
BRINGE UNS, HERR, WIEDER ZU DIR P.

Moderato 3/4, 59 meas. D maj.

MANUSCRIPT. NAZARETH. Holograph — B, Vlo I/II, Vla, Vlc.; later — 3 S, 3 A, 2 T, B and Fl.

BRINGT DEM HERREN FROHE LIEDER P.

Allegro 2/2, 117 meas. F maj.

MANUSCRIPT. C pr., C sec., A, B, "Ob. oder Clar." I/II in C, Co. I/II in F, Vlo I/II, Vla, Vlc., Org.; add. parts — 3 C pr., 2 C sec., 2 A, and later.

HALLELUJAH, DER HEILAND LEBT P.

Allegro 3/4, 160 meas. C maj.

MANUSCRIPT. BETHLEHEM — 3 C pr.. 2 A, T, B, 2 Clarini in C, Vlo I/II, Vla, Vlc., Org.; add. — C pr., and later.
NAZARETH — C, A, T, B, Clarino I/II, Vlo I/II, Vla, Vlc., Org.; add. — Co. I/II in C, S and A. Several later parts.

ICH DANKE DIR AUF MEINEN KNIEN P.

Duetto. Moderato 2/2, 60 meas. B fl. maj.

MANUSCRIPT. Holograph parts — C sec., Clar. I/II in B fl., Fag., Vlo I/II, Vla, Vlc., Org.; add. — Co. in B fl., and C sec.

KINDLEIN, BLEIBET BEI JESU CHRIST P.

Andante 2/2, 25 meas. (Prel., solo and postl.), and 32 (tutti). G maj.

MANUSCRIPT. 3 C pr., 2 C sec., 2 A, B, Vlo I/II, Vla, B.; add. — C sec., and later.

MACHT HOCH DIE THÜR, DIE THOR MACHT WEIT P.

Allegro 2/2, 73 meas. D maj.

MANUSCRIPTS.

BETHLEHEM. 3 C, 2 A, 2 T, 2 B, Clarino I/II in D, Vlo I/II, Vla, Vlc., Org.; add. — C, and later.

NAZARETH. C, A, T, B, Clarino I/II, Vlo I/II, Vla, B, Org.; Co. I/II by Bechler.

SCHALLT UNSERS DANKES FROHE LIEDER P.

Allegro 3/4, 25 twice 25, and 85 meas.

MANUSCRIPT. 3 S, 3 A, T, B, Org. Other parts missing.

SIEHE, ICH VERKÜNDIGE EUCH GROSSE FREUDE P.

Allegro C. Soprano solo, 50 meas.; Coro 3/4, 66 meas. D maj.
Starting with an effective crescendo. A Cembalo is mentioned as keyboard instrument.

MANUSCRIPT. 2 CS, 3 S, 4 C sec., T, B, "Fl. o Ob." I/II, Fag. I/II, Clarino I/II in D, Vlo I/II, Vla, Vlc., Cembalo.; add. —2 S, and later.

UNSER HERZ UND MUND SOLL IHN ERHEBEN P.

Duett. Allegro 2/2, 121 meas. Chor 3/4, twice 29 meas. D maj.

MANUSCRIPT. C pr., C sec., A, B, Co. I/II in D, Vlo I/II, Vla, Vlc., Org. A second Org., for Choral section only. Add. parts by TILL — 2 C pr., C sec., complete, 2 C pr., C sec., choral section only, T, B. Till apparently performed the first section also with the chorus.

UNSER LOOS IST SCHÖN UND GROSS P.

2/2, 42 meas. B fl. maj.
A short anthem, related in style to the following ariettas.

MANUSCRIPT. 5 C pr., 3 C sec., 3 A, B, Vlo I/II, Vla, Vlc., Org.; add. — parts by TILL and later.

Ariettas

DU SÜNDERFREUND! WER VOR DIR WEINT P.

2/4, 4 and three times 20 meas. E fl. maj.

MANUSCRIPT. 3 C pr., 3 C sec., 3 A, B, Vlo I/II, Vla, Vlc., Org.

GOTT SEY DIR GNÄDIG! O DU BEGLÜCKTE KNABEN-SCHAAR P.

Affettuoso 3/4, 80 meas. F maj.

Although written out in full, this composition which is the most touching Michael accomplished, consists of 4 meas. prelude. 16 meas. solo, a choral ritornello of 8 meas. and a repetition of the prelude only. The refrain to the words *Gott sey dir gnädig*, reminds one of the old litany.

MANUSCRIPT. C pr., 4 C pr., 2 Coro, C sec., A, B, Vlo I/II, Vla, B, Org.

HOW BRIGHT APPEARS THE MORNING-STAR P.

Choralmässig C, twice 6 meas., and 10 meas. F maj.

In the character of a hymn. Why Michael should have attempted to replace the classical chorale on the same text, is hard to understand.

MANUSCRIPT. 4 C pr., 2 C sec., 2 A, 2 B, Vlo I/II, Vla. Vlc., Org.; add. — parts later.

JESUS NIMMT SICH UNSRER AN P.

3/8, 4 and twice 36 meas. F maj.

MANUSCRIPT. 4 C pr., 2 C sec., A, B, Vlo I/II, Vla, Vlc., Org.; add. — C sec.

Compositions for Wind Instruments

PARTHIA I.

(Clarinetto Primo e Secondo, Fagotto, Corni e Tromba)

Allegro 3/4. Andante 6/8. Presto 2/4. E fl. maj.

PARTHIA II.

(Clarinetto Primo e Secondo, Fagotto, Corni e Flauto)

Allegro 2/2. Andante 3/4. Menuetto 3/4, with Trio c min. Allegro 2/4, Presto 3/8. E fl. maj.

PARTHIA III.

(Clarinetto Primo e Secundo, Fagotto Primo e Secundo, e Corni)

Grave 3/4. Allegro 3/4. Andante C. Allegro 2/4. E fl. maj.

PARTHIA IV.
(a Due Clarinetti, Due Corni & Due Fagotti)
Allegro C. Andante 6/8, B fl. maj. Presto 2/4. E fl. maj.

PARTHIA V.
(a Due Clarinetti, Due Corni & Due Fagotti)
Allegro C. Andante 2/4, B fl. maj. Menuetto 3/4, with Trio
B fl. maj. Allegro 2/4, with section in c min. E fl. maj.

PARTHIA VI.
(Clarinetto Primo e Secundo, Fagotto Primo
e Secundo, e Corni)
Andante 3/4, Allegro assai 3/4. Andante poco Adagio. Men-
uett 3/4, with Trio. Rondo Allegretto 2/4, with Minore, d min.
F maj.

PARTHIA VII.
(Clarinetto Primo & Secondo, Corno Primo
& Secondo, & Fagotto)
Tempo March C. Andante 6/8, E fl. maj. Menuetto 3/4, with
Trio. C maj. Presto 2/4. c min.

PARTHIA VIII.
(Clarinetto Primo & Secondo, Corno Primo
& Secondo, & Fagotto)
Allegro C. Andante 2/4, E fl. maj. Menuetto, with Trio. A fl.
maj. Allegro assai 2/4, with Majore, C maj. c min.

PARTHIA IX.
This Parthia is preserved neither at Bethlehem nor at Lititz.

PARTHIA X.
(Clarinetto Primo e Secundo, Fagotto Primo
e Secundo, e Corni)
Adagio 3/4. Allegro C. Menuett Grazioso 3/4, with Trio.
Presto 2/4; E fl. maj.

PARTHIA XI.
(Clarinetto Primo e Secundo, Fagotto Primo e Secundo,
Corni e Clarino)
Allegro 3/4. Andante 6/8, B fl. maj. Menuett 3/4, with Trio,
c min. Presto C. E fl. maj.

PARTHIA XII.

(Clarinetto Primo e Secundo, Fagotto Primo e Secundo,
e Corni)

Allegro C. Andante 2/4. Menuetto Allegretto 3/4, with Trio,
d min. Presto 2/4, with section in B fl. maj. F maj.

PARTHIA XIII.

(Clarinetto Primo e Secundo, Fagotto, e Corni)

Allegro C. Adagio 6/8, B fl. maj. Allegro 2/4. E fl. maj.

PARTHIA XIV.

(Clarinetto Primo e Secundo, Fagotto, e Corni)

Allegro moderato C. Allegro assai C. Andante poco Adagio
3/4. Menuett 3/4, with Trio. Allegro 2/4. E fl. maj.

MANUSCRIPTS. The following manuscripts are complete,
including one separate part for each instrument mentioned in
the titles, except the Tromba to Parthia XI in the Lititz manuscript. The clarinet parts are written in B fl., the horns mostly
in E fl., for Parthia III in B fl., for Parthia VI in F, the Tromba
to Parthia I and XI in E fl.

LITITZ. Parthias III, VI and X, VII and VIII, XI and XII,
XIII and XIV, copied in the same, not identified handwriting.
Parthias I and II copied by Bechler. Parthias IV and V copied
by Peter. The horns to Parthia III also in a second copy, transposed as Corni in E fl.

BETHLEHEM. "Michael's and other Parthien or Harmony
Music," Grider's title to a set of bound parts which include, in
addition to copies of European compositions, Michael's Parthien
VII and VIII, and X to XIV, in H. Weber's hand.

SUITEN

für 2 Clarinetten, 2 Hörner u. 2 Fagotts
Bestimmt zu einer Wasserfahrt auf der Lecha
aufgesetzt und zugeeignet seinem Freunde

John Samuel Krause von David Moritz Michael

Bethlm d. 21ten April 1809

No 1. March C, E fl. maj. No 2. Andantino C, E fl. maj. No 3.
Menuett 3/4, E fl. maj. No 4. Allegro C, E fl. maj. No 5. Adagio
2/4, B fl. maj. No 6. Presto 3/8. Chorale-mässig, A fl. maj.
Da capo senza repl. No. 7. Echo Allegretto 2/4, E fl. maj. No. 8.
Menuett Allegretto 3/4, E fl. maj. Zusammenruf C, E fl. maj.
No 9. Retour March, Vivace, E fl. maj. No 10. Polonese 3/4. E fl.
maj. No 11. Rondo Vivace 2/4, E fl. maj., with minore c min.

No 12. Adagio C, B fl. maj.; Waldstück für 2 Hörner by der Springe zu blasen. No 13. Menuett Allegretto 3/4, E fl. maj., with Trio c min. No 14. Andante 6/8, Allegro 2/4, Presto 3/8. Andante d. C. senza repl. No 15. Finale Choral-mässig C, E fl. maj.

MANUSCRIPT. BETHLEHEM. Holograph parts — Clar. I/II in B fl., Fag. I/II, Co. I/II in E fl. The chorales apparently are composed by Michael himself. This composition is mentioned in O. Sonneck's Bibliography of Early American Secular Music.

SUITEN

Bey einer Quelle zu blasen

Introductio C. *NB. Dieses Stück wird 3 mal geblasen 1.) von den Hörnern allein. 2.) mit Hörner und Fagott. 3.) mit Hörner, Fagott und Clarinetten.*

Pars 1. E fl. maj.
Allegro moderato C. Andante 6/8. Menuett 3/4. Presto 2/4.

Pars 2. B fl. maj.
Pastorale 6/8. Menuett 3/4. Arioso 2/4, F maj. Presto 3/8, with middle section.

Pars 3. E fl. maj.
Allegro moderato C. Menuett 3/8, with Trio, Andante Coren solo. Adagio 3/4. B fl. maj. Presto 2/4-3/8.

MANUSCRIPT. BETHLEHEM. Copy by H W in another set of bound parts to various compositions for wind-instruments — Clar. I/II in B fl., Fag., Co. I/II in E fl. The first page of Clar. I to Par 3. is reproduced in the present catalogue, plate V. This part apparently represents Michael's picture of the whirls of the Lehigh, and the fear of the musicians, with the subsequent thanks for the rescue from danger. The Allegro includes Michael's best piece of composition, but still it may scarcely be called more than modest.

JOHANN CHRISTIAN BECHLER

Johann Christian Bechler was born on the Island of Oesel, in the Baltic Sea, on Jan. 7, 1784. He came to America in 1806, and became one of the first professors of the newly founded theological seminary, then at Nazareth. In 1812, he was ordained a deacon and moved to Philadelphia, then to Staten Island. He was principal of Nazareth Hall from 1817 to 1822, then pastor and principal of Linden Hall at Lititz. From 1829 to 1835, he lived in the Southern province. Consecrated a bishop in 1835, he went back to Europe in the following year, served the Russian congregations, centering in Sarepta, Astrachan, for a number of years, and died at Herrnhuth, April 15, 1857.

Bechler has written a greater number of compositions than any of the later Moravians in America. These compositions fall into two groups, a series of larger anthems, and another one, of short hymns, ariettas. The latter are unpretending and display occasionally a nice melody. The anthems, on the other hand, are mostly of a much larger scope than most of the compositions written in America before Bechler's arrival. Not much can be said in their favor as they are made up with the most common patterns. The titles of 11 compositions which could not be located are found in the *Catalogus der Kirchen-Music der Gemeine in Graceham. Neuspausgefertiget den 1sten Decr. 1831.*

Bechler composed, in addition to his anthems, the liturgies No. 44, *Osterliturgie*, 48, *Zur Himmelfahrt*, 51, *Lobgesang zum Andenken der Märtyrer*, 55, *Zum Engelfest*, and, according to a note by Till the liturgies No. 80 and 82 which could not be located.

Anthems

BRINGE UNS, HERR, WIEDER ZU DIR P.

4 Voci, 2 Violini, Viola, Fondamento.

Langsam 3/4, 82 meas. F maj.

Copy — Bethlehem, together with *Kommt, ach kommt, ihr Gnadenkinder*. Org. part missing.

DANK, ANBETUNG, LOB UND EHRE P.

4 Voci, 2 Violini, Viola, Violoncello, 2 Flauti, 2 Corni in Es (E fl.), 2 Clarini & Organo.

A maestoso is three times followed by a section of different character, first by a S solo with following tutti, Andante, then by an Allegretto sotto voce, finally by a Piu vivo. 174 meas. E fl. maj.

Copies — Bethlehem, with a date, 1808, and Lititz. The latter by Herbst, No. 126, with a holograph. Clarino, and add. parts, including a Fag. In Lancaster and Graceham catalogues.

DIE GNADE DES HERRN JESU CHRIST P.

4 Voci, 2 Violini, Viola, Violoncello, 2 Clarinetti, 2 Fagotti, 2 Corni (in E fl.), Organo.
Feyerlich 2/2, 74 meas. E fl. maj.
Copies — Bethlehem and Lititz. The latter by Herbst, No. 138, with single parts by Wolle.

ER WISCHT DIE TRÄNLEIN AB P. — HE WIPES AWAY OUR TEARS P.

4 Voci, 2 Violini, Viola, Fundamento, Organo.
Affettuoso 3/4, 126 meas.
Holograph parts — Nazareth, with add. Fl.

GOTT ISTS, DER IN EUCH WIRKET P.

4 Voci, 2 Violini, Viola, Fondamento, 2 Corni (in E fl.), Organo.
A Grave C, of 10 meas., is twice followed by an Andante 3/4, of 24 meas., the second being followed by a section of 32 meas. E fl. maj.
Copies — Bethlehem and Lititz. The latter by Herbst, No. 150.

GOTT WAR IN CHRISTO P.

4 Voci, 2 Violini, Viola, Violoncello, Flauto ad lib., Corni I/II (in E fl.), Organo.
Moderato C, 60 meas. E fl. maj.
Holograph parts — Bethlehem, together with *Ich will dem Herrn singen.*

GROSS IST DER HERR UND HOCHBERÜHMT P.

4 Voci, 2 Violini, Viola, Violoncello, 2 Clarini (in C), 2 Corni (in C), 2 Flauti o Clarinetti (in C), Organo.
Allegro maestoso. 115 meas. C maj. The composition is also handed down with a second text *Jauchzt und lobsingt p.* with slightly different Clarino parts.
Holograph parts — Nazareth, together with *Sey Lob und Ehr p.*
Copies— Bethlehem and Lititz, the former by Peter, the latter by Herbst, No. 137. In Lancaster and Graceham catalogues.

HALLELUJAH, PREIS, EHR UND MACHT P.

4 Voci, 2 Violini, Viola, Violoncello, 2 Flauti, 2 Clarinetti (in B fl.), 2 Fagotti, 2 Corni (in C), 2 Clarini (in C), Organo.

Allegro moderato, 173 meas. C maj.

Holograph parts — Nazareth. Copy — Bethlehem.

ICH WILL DEM HERREN SINGEN P.

4 Voci, 2 Violini, Viola, Violoncello, Flauto obligato, 2 Corni (in C), Organo.

Allegretto 2/4, 133 meas. C maj.

Holograph parts — Bethlehem, together with *Gott war in Christo*. In Lancaster catalogue.

KOMM, O KOMM, DU GEIST DER LIEBE P.

4 Voci, 2 Violini, Viola, Violoncello, Organo.

Larghetto 3/4, 62 meas. B fl. maj.

According to Till *Zum 13n August 1827 Componirt von J. C. Bechler.*

Copies — Bethlehem, together with *Siehe, ich habe vor dir gegeben* — Lititz, late, together with Michael's *Unser Loos ist schön und gross.*

KOMMT, ACH KOMMT, IHR GNADENKINDER P.

4 Voci, 2 Violini, Viola, Fondamento, Corni I/II (in E fl.).

Lebhaft, 76 meas. E fl. maj.

Copies — Bethlehem, with Org. by Wolle — Lititz, by Herbst, No. 150, together with *Gott ists, der in euch wirket.*

LASSET UNS DEN HERREN PREISEN P.

Zum 7ten Sept. 1810 meinem lieben Bruder Johann Friedr. Peter freundschaftlichst gwidmet von Joh. Chr. Bechler

Allegro con spirito C, 141 meas. D maj.

Only composition by Bechler handed down in a holograph score, from Lancaster. It is accompanied by a letter, dated *Nazareth den 3ten Sept. 1810,* in which Bechler explains that he would have wanted to send Peter a composition for his birthday, as Peter had done the year before, but that he was detained at that time, and that therefore he was sending Peter a piece to celebrate the *Chorfest.* The score includes, on 11 staves, Clarini in D, Corni in D, Flauti, Violino I, Violino II, Viola, S, A, T, B, and Fondam. The last is figured.

Holograph parts — Bethlehem.

LOB SEY DIR, HERR ALLER DINGE P.

4 Voci, 2 Violini, Viola, Violoncello, 2 Clarinetti (in B fl.), 2 Corni, 2 Clarini, Organo.

Moderato 2/2, 145 meas. C maj.

Holograph parts — Bethlehem, together with *Preis und Dank und Ehre p.* — Lititz, and Nazareth, the last set not complete.

PREIS UND DANK UND EHRE P.

4 Voci, 2 Violini, Viola, Violoncello, 2 Oboi, è Clarinetti (in C), 2 Corni (in D), 2 Clarini (in C), Organo.

Allegro pomposo 2/2, 123 meas. D maj.

Holograph parts — Bethlehem, including the preceding and the present number. Incomplete set of parts, partly holograph — Nazareth, with title *Praises, thanks and adoration oder Preis und Dank.* In Graceham catalogue, with similar indication.

SEY LOB UND EHR DEM HÖCHSTEN GUT P.

4 Voci, 2 Violini, Viola, Violoncello, 2 Oboes, 2 Corni (in D). 2 Clarini (in D), Timpani, Organo.

Allegro maestoso, 132 meas. D maj.

Copies — Bethlehem and Lititz, the latter by Herbst, No. 135. In Lancaster and Graceham catalogues.

SIEHE, ICH HABE VOR DIR GEGEBEN EINE OFFENE THÜR P.

4 Voci, 2 Violini, Viola, Violoncello, Organo.

Grave 2/2, frey recitirt doch tactmässig, S solo, 12 meas. D maj. Coro Andante 3/4, 17 meas. Grave solo, 11 meas. Andante 3/4, Coro, 14 meas. A maj.

Two copies — Bethlehem, one with date *13. Aug. 27.* Copy of the solo sections only — Lititz.

UNSRE SEEL SOLL DICH ERHEBEN P.

4 Voci, 2 Violini, Viola, Violoncello, 2 Flauti, 2 Corni (in D). 2 Clarini (in D), Organo.

Allegro maestoso 2/2, 116 meas. D maj.

Copies — Bethlehem and Lititz, the latter by Herbst, No. 137. In Lancaster and Graceham catalogues.

WIR HALTEN DAS FEST MIT FREUDEN P.

4 Voci, 2 Violini, Viola, Violoncello, 2 Clarini (in D), Organo.
Lebhaft 3/4, 64 meas. Langsam Solo, 34 meas. Tempo I, 60
meas. D maj.
Copies — Bethlehem and Lititz, the latter much later.

Ariettas

FAITHFUL CHRIST OUR SHEPHERD IS P.

Canto primo e secondo, Basso, 2 Violini, Viola, Violoncello,
Organo.
Vivace 2/2, 12 meas. 3 verses. D maj.
Copy — Bethlehem. In Graceham catalogue.

GESALBETER HEILAND VERORDNET ZUM SEGNEN P.

4 Voci, 2 Violini, Viola, Violoncello, 2 Clarinetti (in B fl.),
Fagotto, 2 Corni (in E fl.), Organo.
Affetuoso. 32 meas. 2 verses. E fl. maj.
Copy — Bethlehem.

O JESU CHRIST, DEIN KRIPPLEIN IST P.

4 Voci, 2 Violini, Viola, Violoncello, Organo.
Innig und fröhlich, 2/4, 16 meas. 5 verses. C maj.
Copy by Peter — Bethlehem.

O, WAS WANDELT UNSRE SEELEN ÜBER JESU
LEIDEN AN P.

4 Voci, 2 Violini, Viola, Violoncello, Organo.
Affettuoso C, 16 meas. 2 verses. E fl. maj. Also with beginning
Ach, was wandelt p.
Copy by Peter — Bethlehem. In Lancaster catalogue.

O WIE WIRDS SO WOHL THUN P.

4 Voci, 2 Violini, Viola, Violoncello, Organo.
Vivace C, 24 meas. 4 verses. C maj.
Copies — Bethlehem and Lititz. In Lancaster catalogue.

PRAISE THE LORD, GOD OUR SALVATION P.

Pomposo C, 8 meas. C maj.
Copy of C pr. I and Org. only — Lititz. In Lancaster catalogue.

SELIGE GEMEINE, JESUS SEGNE DICH P.
4 Voci, 2 Violini, Viola, Violoncello, Organo.
Andantino 2/2, 17 meas. 2 verses. C maj.
Copy by Peter, following his *Das Heiligthum ist aufgethan* — Bethlehem; another — Lititz. In Lancaster and Graceham catalogues.

SING HALLELUJAH, PRAISE THE LORD P.
4 Voci, 2 Violini, Viola, Violoncello, Organo.
2/2, 16 meas. 2 verses. B fl. maj. Also with the text *We too unite in songs to laud p.*
Copy — Bethlehem. In Graceham catalogue. Printed in Wolle's tune book and the Moravian Hymnbook.

TO GOD OUR IMMANUEL MADE FLESH AS WE ARE P.
4 Voci, 2 Violini, Viola, Violoncello, 2 Clarini (in D), Organo.
Vivace 3/4, 27 meas. D maj.
Copy, incomplete — Bethlehem.

WEIL ICH JESU SCHÄFLEIN BIN P. or JESUS MAKES MY HEART REJOICE P.
Soprano solo, 2 Violini, Viola, Violoncello, Organo.
Freudig or Cheerful (sic!) C, 12 meas. 3 verses. E fl. maj.
Copy, partly by Peter, incomplete? — Bethlehem.

Compositions for Wind Instruments
PARTHIA
2 Clarinetti (in B fl.), Fagotto, 2 Corni (in E fl.), Clarino (in E fl.).
Allegro con spirito 2/2. Allegretto 3/4, con (3) Variazioni, B fl. maj. Menuetto 3/4, with Trio. Presto 2/4. E fl. maj.
Holograph parts — Lititz.

MARCHES
For 2 Clarinetts, 2 Horns, 1 Bassoon and 1 Trumpet.
In a collection of 12 Marches, the Nos. II and VII are marked as being *di Bechler*. Both consist of 2 sections of 8 meas. each, and are in E fl. maj. Others included are by Türk, Rolle, Gebhard. Two are called Buonaparte's March. The last one is Washington's March.
Manuscript — Lititz. In the same handwriting as Michael's Parthien Nos. II, VI-VIII, and X to XIV.

PETER RICKSECKER

Peter Ricksecker was born at Bethlehem, 1791. He attended the Seminary at Nazareth, then became teacher there. He worked subsequently at Lancaster, and then, ordained a deacon in 1826, as missionary in the West Indies. He retired in 1857, and died at Bethlehem, 1873. He played the violin and organ, sang tenor, and composed. His compositions, apparently under the influence of Bechler, are not important. Ricksecker compiled the *Catalogus der zur Gemeine in Lancaster gehörigen Gemein-Stücke, 1830,* which mentions four compositions by Ricksecker himself, three of which are lost. Ricksecker also composed a *Battle of New Orleans,* an extremely dull piece of programme music for the pianoforte.

DU WIRST LUST HABEN AM HERRN P.

4 Voci, 2 Violini, Viola, Violoncello, Organo.

Andante Grazioso 3/4, 68 meas. F maj.

Holograph parts — Nazareth. In Graceham catalogue, compiled 1831.

LOB SEY DIR, HERR ALLER DINGE P.

Moderato 2/2. C maj.

Incomplete set of parts by Bechler — Nazareth. A note on the Org. indicates that the composition was *con Clarinetti e Corni.*

O SÜSSE SEELENWEIDE P.

4 Voci, 2 Violini, Viola, Violoncello, 2 Flauti(?), Organo.

Andantino con affetto, 2/2, 61 meas. F maj.

Copy, including Fl. I, but no Fl. II — Nazareth.

PRAISES, THANKS AND ADORATION P. — PREIS UND DANK UND EHRE P.

Allegro pomposo C. D maj.

Incomplete set of parts by Bechler — Nazareth.

SING PRAISES UNTO GOD P.

4 Voci, 2 Violini, Viola, Violoncello, 2 Flauti, 2 Corni (in D), Trumpet (in D), Organo.

Allegro C, 109 meas. D maj.

Copy — Lititz. In Lancaster and Graceham catalogues.

PETER WOLLE

Peter Wolle was the son of a missionary, born at New Herrn-hut, St. Thomas, West Indies, in 1792. In 1800, he entered Naz-areth Hall. He was one of three students when the Theological Seminary at Nazareth was opened. He served as minister sub-sequently at Lancaster, Philadelphia and Lititz. In 1845 he was consecrated a bishop. He died at Bethlehem in 1871.

Wolle must have been a pupil of Michael and, later on, of Bechler who mentions the fact that he helped others in composi-tion. Wolle learned to write clean settings, but in general, he relied rather on common patterns than on his imagination. Most of his compositions apparently were written at a comparatively early date.

Wolle was the editor of the *Moravian Tune Book Arranged for four voices with accompaniment for Organ and Piano To which are added Chants for the Church Litany and a Number of Ap-proved Anthems* first published in 1836. This is the first Mor-avian Tune Book printed in America, and, at the same time, the first one clearly indicating the parts for a four-part chorus. Wolle included an anthem of his own composition, *Sing Hallelu-jah, Christ doth live*, for 2 Trebles and Bass with Organ.

In addition to the compositions by Wolle listed below, we may mention a duet, *If that high world, Written by Lord Byron, Com-posed by Revd. Peter Wolle*, which was published by J. G. Klemm in Philadelphia, and a Coro, *Happy soul thy days are ended*, an Arietta which was written for the funeral of the *Widowed Sister Rosina Luckenbach*, on Nov. 6, 1862.

Anthems

COME JOYFUL HALLELUJAH RAISE P.

4 Voci, 2 Violini, Viola, Violoncello, 2 Flutes (in D fl. !), 2 Corni (in E fl.), 2 Clarini (in E fl.), Organo.

Allegro moderato 3/4, 171 meas. E fl. maj.

An Anthem for the Fourth of July. The text ends *O tune thy harp, and strike thy lay America, Columbia*.

Holograph parts — Bethlehem. Late copy, with add. Trom-bone, Cornett — Lititz.

DER HERR IST GROSS P.

4 Voci, 2 Violini, Viola, Violoncello, 2 Flauti, 2 Corni (in C), 2 Clarini (in C), Organo.

Allegro moderato C, 109 meas. C maj.

Holograph parts — Nazareth. Partly holograph set of parts *Zum Friedens-Dank-Fest den 13ten April 1815*, following J. A. P. Schulz's hymn *Herr unser Gott sey hoch gepreiset* — Bethlehem.

ES IST EIN KÖSTLICH DING, DEM HERREN DANKEN P.

4 Voci, 2 Violini, Viola, Violoncello, 2 Flauti, 2 Corni (in G), Organo.

Munter 2/2, 100 meas. G maj.

Holograph parts — Nazareth. Copy — Bethlehem.

FÜR MICH, O HERR, MEIN GOTT UND HEILAND P.

8 Voci, 2 Violini, Viola, Violoncello, Organo.

Grave C, 75 meas. E fl. maj.

Wolle's only composition for a double chorus known. By far his finest and most personal work. It is included in the series Music of the American Moravians, No. 11.

Holograph parts — Bethlehem.

SCHMECKE UND ERFAHRE P.

4 Voci, 2 Violini, Viola, Violoncello e Organo.

Andante 3/4, 96 meas. A maj.

Holograph parts — Bethlehem.

WIEDERHOLTS MIT FROHEN TÖNEN P.

4 Voci, 2 Violini, Viola, Violoncello, 2 Flauti, 2 Corni (in D), 2 Clarini (in D), Organo.

Allegro moderato C, 110 meas. D maj.

Partly holograph set of parts — Lititz. Copy — Bethlehem.

Compositions for Wind Instruments

MADISON'S MARCH

2 Clarinetts, 2 Horns (in E fl.), Fagotto, Flute and Tromba (in E fl.).

2/2, 16 and 24 meas. E fl. maj.

A collection of pieces for wind-instruments, written by John Levering includes the present composition together with Menuet Militaire by Boccherini, and the Battle of Maringo di Viguerie, the latter consisting of Clarino solo, March, Fanfare and two Rondeaus.

FRANCIS FLORENTINE HAGEN

Francis F. Hagen was born at Salem, North Carolina, October 30, 1815. He was educated first at Salem, then in Nazareth Hall, finally at the Theological Seminary at Nazareth. He worked as teacher in Salem, then at Nazareth Hall. In 1844, he was ordained to the ministry, and served several places in the Southern Province, then York, Pa., New Dorp, Staten Island, N. Y., and Harmony, Iowa. Injured in an accident, he was forced to retire, and devoted his time to literary and musical pursuits, the former resulting in his *Old Landmarks, or Faith and Practice of the Moravian Church at the Time of its Revival and Restoration in 1727 and twenty years after,* the latter in the series *Church and Home Organist's Companion. A choice selection of voluntaries Consisting of Anthems, Reveries, Transcriptions of well-known Hymn Tunes, Prayers, Marches, etc.,* published by Fred. Williams, Philadelphia. Lee & Walker, Philadelphia, in 1854 published *ALMA MATER. Ode on the removal of the old School building of Salem Female Academy, North Carolina, and the Erection of the new . . . Words and music by the Revd. F. F. Hagen.* Hagen died at Lititz on July 7, 1907.

Hagen undoubtedly was the most gifted among the later American Moravian composers. He had an exceptional sense for distinguished popular melody. He composed, in addition to the earlier works listed below, four anthems and the Doxology, *Unto the Lamb that was slain,* in 1879 and 1880 for the Bethlehem congregation. An Overture by Hagen is found in a set of bound partbooks including similar works by various composers. It was presumably written before Hagen left the Northern Province for the second time, in 1844. It antedates, in any case, the anthem just mentions for it is included in R. A. Grider's catalogue of the library of the Philharmonic Society of Bethlehem compiled 1873.

ZWEY STÜCKE

No. 1. SCHLAF, LIEBES KIND, MIT DER GEMEINE JESU FRIEDEN P.

4 Voci, 2 Violini, Viola, Violoncello, Organo.
Adagio 2/2, 42 meas. E fl. maj.

No. 2. SELGE LEBENS-STUNDEN P.

4 Voci, 2 Violini, Viola, Violoncello, Organo.
Langsam 3/4, 64 meas. B fl. maj.

Both compositions handed down in a copy by Till, with the date 1834 for the first. They are rather stiff, and presumably were composed at about the same time.

BIS DEREINST MEIN STÜNDLEIN SCHLÄGT P.

4 Voci, 2 Violini, Viola, Violoncello, Organo.
Larghetto 2/4. 50 meas. a min. 28 meas. A maj.

This quite attractive and expressive composition concludes the series Music of the American Moravians. It emulates in its first section the series of suspensions cherished at the beginning of the 18th century. The copy preserved was written by Till, who died in 1844. The composition itself presumably dates back to the late thirties.

MORGENSTERN, AUF FINSTRE NACHT P. — MORNING STAR, O CHEERING SIGHT P.

2/2, 15 meas. B fl. maj.

This charming Arietta which became a standing feature in the Christmas service of the Moravian Church, is said to have been composed at Salem, in 1842. It is based on alternating solo and tutti. Originally written for children's voices with organ accompaniment, it was published in the Moravian Hymnbook *(The Liturgy and the Offices of Worship and Hymns of the American Province of the Unitas Fratrum)*, in a version for mixed chorus, transposed into A fl. maj., and augmented by a full measure through doubling the value of the notes in the final cadence. Copies of the original version are preserved at Bethlehem and Lititz.

CANTATA. HERR WIE SIND DEINE WERKE SO GROSS UND VIEL P.

4 Voci, 2 Violini, Viola, Violoncello e Basso, 2 Flauti, 2 Clarinetti (in C), 2 Corni (in C), 2 Clarini (in C), Fagotto e Trombone basso, Organo.

Maestoso 2/2, 21 meas. Allegro moderato 2/2, 39 meas. Andante 2/2, 33 meas. Allegro 2/2, 78 meas. C maj.

This composition, which is handed down in a copy by Till, is by far the most extended sacred composition written by an American Moravian. Till indicates that it was composed by *Fr. Hagen, Professor in Nazareth Hall*. The composition is amateurish in various respects, but includes many excellent details. The first movement and the end of the last, for the full chorus, are well sustained and harmonically interesting. The second movement is fugal, with continuous modulations. The third movement is attributed to single voices, evidently soli. The fourth movement starts with a second fugato. The character of the composition makes it probable that it was one of Hagen's early attempts at composing, and that it was written before Hagen came to the Northern Province for the second time. The first page of the organ part is reproduced in this catalogue, plate W.

ADDENDA
Compositions by Various Authors

SIMON PETER

Simon Peter was a son of the older Johann Friedrich Peter, and a brother of John Frederick Peter, the musician. He was born at Heerendyk, Holland, on April 2, 1743. He came to America in 1770, evidently together with his brother. He first served as teacher at Nazareth Hall where Till was one of his pupils. Then he came to Bethlehem where he taught David Weinland to play the double bass. In 1784 he went to North Carolina. He spent the rest of his life as minister of various congregations in the Southern Province. He died at Salem, May 29, 1819. He was married four times.

A single composition by Simon Peter only is handed down in the Northern Province, the Arietta *O Anblick, der mirs Herze bricht p.* This Solo for a Soprano with strings and organ, Affectuoso 2/4, 32 meas., c min., is a remarkable composition, original and expressive. It was copied by John Frederick Peter, and is included in the first volume of the series Music of the American Moravians.

The earliest Bethlehem catalogue mentions two compositions by Simon Peter, *O Chor des Herrn p.*, which is, we may assume, erroneously attributed to Simon instead of Johann Friedrich, and *Kommt herzu und lasset uns dem Herren p.* Two other compositions, *Die Gottes Seraphim p.* and *Siehe meine Knechte sollen essen p.* are mentioned in a catalogue from Salem.

JOHANN GEBHARD CUNOW

Johann Gebhard Cunow was born at Halenberg an der Priegnitz, on January 6, 1760. He came to America in 1796, as administrator of the property of the Church. Trying to apply autocratic methods, he made himself thoroughly disliked, and was called back in 1822. He died in Königsberg, 1829.

One composition by Cunow is preserved, and it would seem that he never attempted to write another one. The composition in question is a solo, with strings and organ, Langsam, mit Empfindung 3/4, 33 meas. F maj. It is handed down with three different texts, *O Jesu nimm zum Lohn der Schmerzen*, which appears in a copy dated 1799, *O sel'ges Loos dem meine Seele oft sehnsuchtsvoll entgegen blickt p.* and *Geliebtes Kind, Dein Loos ist köstlich p.* The last one is said to have been written by Cunow for the funeral of one of his daughters.

JOHN FREDERICK FRÜAUFF

John Frederick Früauff, baptized Johann Friedrich, was born at Neudietendorf in 1762. He came to America in 1791, was ordained a deacon, and served as chaplain of the single brethren at Lititz. He served subsequently at various places, including Bethlehem, Philadelphia and Nazareth. He was principal of the Boarding School at Lititz from 1805 to 1815, and later on Principal of the Boarding School at Bethlehem for a few years. He died at Bethlehem on November 14, 1839.

Copies of sonatas and other compositions for piano by Haydn and Mozart which Früauff made for his daughter seem to indicate that he was a good pianist himself. Only one composition by him is preserved, the *Advents- und Weihnachts-Liturgie, No. 26.* Probably Früauff has not composed concerted music.

JOHANN LUDWIG HERBST

John Herbst had two sons, one of whom died before him, leaving two children. It is probable that Johann Ludwig Herbst was one of Bishop Herbst's sons; no dates about his life, however, could be found.

Johann Ludwig Herbst left three compositions which are handed down in copies by Johann Herbst and Peter, evidently written not much before or after 1810. One of these, *Freuen und fröhlich müssen seyn p.*, is a regular anthem, for chorus, strings, 2 horns and organ, Vivace C, 88 meas., Langsamer 30 meas., Tempo primo, 54 meas. It exists in two versions, in A maj. and C maj. The other compositions were intended for a child's funeral. The first, *Wenn kleine Himmels Erben p.* is for chorus, strings and organ. Moderato sempre p 3/4, 59 meas., Etwas langsamer, 85 meas. G maj. The other one, *Wenn Kinder die sterbliche Hülle ablegen p* is a solo, Andante C, 85 meas. c min. The last one is slightly more attractive than the others.

CH(ARLES) H(ENR)Y LEVERING

A composition *Wenn ich den Heiland für mich leiden sehe,* Affectuoso 3/4, 86 meas. E fl. maj. for chorus, strings, organ and an add. flute, which is handed down with the Lititz material indicates this name as that of the composer. Nothing could be stated about him.

CHARLES HOMMANN

Charles Hommann, possibly the son of a music publisher at Philadelphia, can be traced as a music teacher in that city from 1828 to 1845. Whether he was a Moravian and how much time he spent at Bethlehem, we do not know. The Bethlehem Archive preserves a

Sinfonia a Due Violini, Alto, Flauto, 2 Oboi, 2 Clarinetti, 2 Corni, Fagotto e Basso. Composed and dedicated to the Philharmonic Society of Bethlehem by Charles Hommann of Philadelphia.

Adagio 2/2—Allegro con brio C.—Andante sostenuto C, B fl. maj.—Menuetto Allegro, with Trio E fl. maj.—Finale Allegro assai C. E fl. maj.

This symphony, the quality of which is not very high, was apparently written in the thirties or early forties. It is presumably one of the first symphonies written by a native American. While Michael scarcely would have ventured to compose anything as elaborate as a symphony, it is quite possible that the existence of the present piece gave birth to the rumor that a symphony by Michael was preserved among the piles of music which originally belonged to the Philharmonic Society of Bethlehem.

PLATES

SELECTED COMPOSITIONS

AND

INTERESTING PAGES

FROM

ORIGINAL MANUSCRIPTS

LIST OF PLATES

A. Title-page to a composition, adapted for the use at the Sister's House, Bethlehem.

B. First of the Canto Primo of J. Dencke's "Doxologie" for the opening of the provincial synod at Bethlehem, 1766. Copy by I. Nitschmann.

C. D. E. The first two pieces from Dencke's Christmas music for the children's choir, Bethlehem 1767. Score by J. F. Peter.

F. G. J. F. Peter's first composition, the solo "Leite mich in Deiner Wahrheit," Nazareth 1770, holograph score Bethlehem 1774.

H. Peter's unique song, for a soprano with an accompanying keyboard-instrument, Bethlehem 1775. Holograph manuscript.

I. J. K. L. Peter's liturgy for weddings, Lititz 1779. Holograph score.

M. N. Peter's Organo obligato to "Nicht uns, Herr, sondern Deinem Namen," composed for Bethlehem between 1790 and 1800.

O. First Violin to Herbst's "Auf, Seele, schicke dich" with variations by Peter; in the latter's handwriting, Bethlehem ca. 1810.

P. Q. R. S. Herbst's organ-part to "Gott hat unter uns aufgerichtet," used and presumably composed for the inauguration of the Bethlehem church, 1806.

T. U. First Violin parts to the two versions of Herbst's "Lobet den Herrn, alle Heiden," the first written by I. Nitschmann, the second by C. G. Schaaff.

V. First clarinet from D. M. Michael's Suiten "Bey einer Quelle zu blasen," including the presumably programmatic section of Pars 3., copied by H. Weber, ca. 1810.

W. First page of the Organ part to F. F. Hagen's Cantata, "Herr, wie sind deine Werke so gross," copied by J. C. Till, ca. 1840.

X. Birthday gratulation, given to Jacob van Vleck in 1795, picturing him while "singing and playing" with a group of sisters or, more probably, girls of the boarding school, the principal of which Van Vleck was at that time. The present plate was made from an old photograph, the original drawing not being preserved.

<del>Lasset uns lobsingen</del>

<del>Die herzlich selige Herz ihr geren</del>

Clavecin
due Harpae
Violino primo
Violino secondo
Viola
Canto 1mo et 2do
Alto, Basso,
et
Violoncello.

Fürs led. Brüder: Haus in Bethlehem.

A

H

B dur.

M

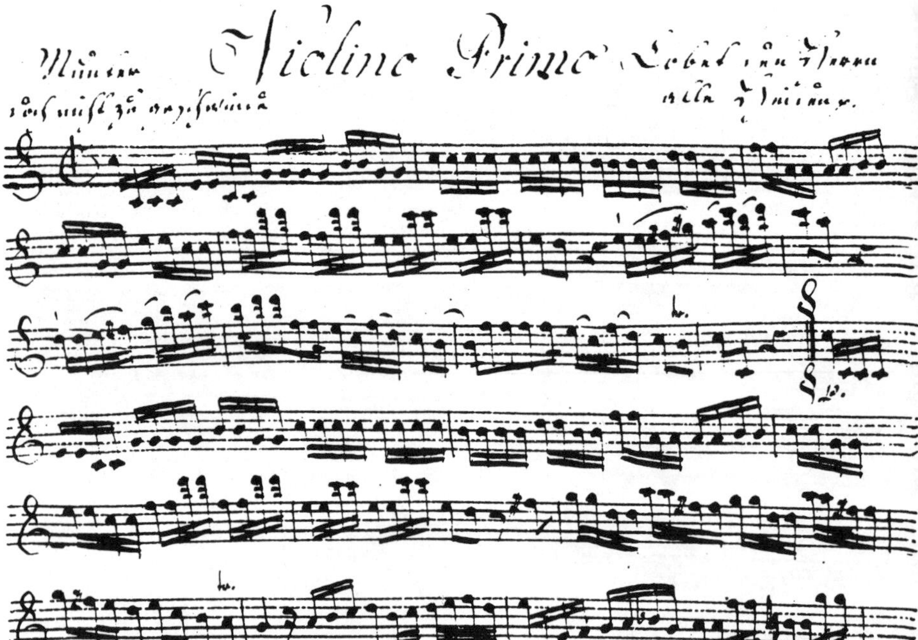

T

V

X